P9-EFI-216

Christianity, Cults & Religions

BEN

ROSE
PUBLISHING

Carson, California

© 2008 Bristol Works, Inc.
Rose Publishing, Inc.
17909 Adria Maru Lane
Carson, California 90746 U.S.A.
Email: info@rose-publishing.com
www.rose-publishing.com

Includes these Rose Publishing Titles:

Christianity, Cults & Religions © 1996, 2000, 2004, 2005 RW Research, Inc.
        Editor: Paul Carden. Contributors: James Bjornstad, PhD; Robert M. Bowman, Jr., MA;
        H. Wayne House, PhD; Eric Pement; Viola Larson
Christianity, Cults & the Occult © 2006 Rose Publishing, Inc.
        Editor: Paul Carden. Contributors: Brooks Alexander; Marcia Montenegro; Eric Pement;
        Marcelo Souza, PhD
Christianity & Eastern Religions © 2008 Bristol Works, Inc.
        Editor: Paul Carden. Author: Mark Albrecht, MA. Contributors: H. L. Richard; J. Isamu
        Yamamoto; Brooks Alexander; András Szalai; James Stephens
Islam & Christianity © 2004, 2013 RW Research, Inc.
        Author: Bruce Green, MA. Contributors: Andras Szalai, PhD
10 Q&A on Jehovah's Witnesses © 2006 RW Research, Inc.
        Editor: Paul Carden. Author: Christy (Harvey) Darlington. Contributors: Robert M. Bowman,
        Jr., MA
10 Q&A on Mormonism © 2006 RW Research, Inc.
        Editor: Paul Carden. Author: Bill McKeever. Contributors: Robert M. Bowman, Jr., MA
10 Keys to Witnessing to Cults © 2008 RW Research, Inc.
        Author: Ron Rhodes, PhD. Contributing Author: Christy (Harvey) Darlington

All Scripture quotations, unless otherwise noted, are taken from the *Holy Bible, New International Version®. NIV®.* Copyright © 1973, 1978, 1984 by International Bible Society. Used by permission of Zondervan. All rights reserved.

Library of Congress Cataloging-in-Publication Data

Christianity, cults & religions.
        p. cm. – (Rose Bible basics)
    ISBN 978-1-59636-202-4 (pbk.)
    1. Christianity and other religions–Miscellanea. I. Title: Christianity, cults, and religions.
    BR127.C47425 2008
    261.2-dc22

                                2008007518

Printed by Regent Publishing Services Ltd.
Hong Kong, China
November 2015, 7th printing

CHRISTIANITY, CULTS & RELIGIONS

Contents

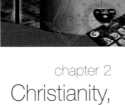
Continued
on next
page
→

CHRISTIANITY, CULTS & RELIGIONS

Contents

Christianity, Cults & Religions

Compare 17 Religions and Cults
with Biblical Christianity

Why should Christians study other religions?
The New Testament offers us two kinds of examples.

First, in Acts 17 the Apostle Paul engages with the non-Christian religions of his day. Paul knows their beliefs well enough to quote their spiritual authorities (see verses 24–28), and his goal is clearly to build bridges to help their followers understand the gospel.

Second, in their epistles Paul, Peter, John, and Jude engage with the counterfeit gospels of their day. In order to warn and instruct Christians about the teachings of false apostles and prophets, these New Testament writers had to be familiar with their claims. The writers' goal is clearly to uphold the faith and defend the flock—and they don't hesitate to identify deceptive and divisive teachers by name when appropriate.

In today's shrinking world, Jesus' followers are faced with more religious groups than ever before. As we seek to engage with cults and world religions constructively and compassionately, the motives and methods of the apostles and the other authors of Scripture are our best model for ministry.

What Other Groups May Teach About Jesus and Biblical Responses:

• Jesus was not God.	(See verses D, I, U, Y)
• Jesus was created by God	(See verses J, M, U)
• There are three separate gods: Father, Son, and Holy Spirit, not one God in three persons.	(A, B, J, Z)
• Jesus is not necessary because there is no sin.	(F, O, P, R)
• Jesus was not raised bodily from the dead.	(C, R, S)
• Jesus was a great prophet, but not God.	(H, J, V)
• There are many ways to God, not just one.	(F, K, X)
• Jesus is not necessary because people must pay for their own sins.	(L, P, Q, T)
• Jesus died for sins, but people can't be saved unless they obey all of the teachings of the church.	(K, Q, T)
• Jesus is God, but less than God the Father.	(H, K, V)
• Jesus was just a man.	(J, E)
• Jesus is not the only son of God.	(F, G, Z)
• Jesus will never come again.	(N, W)

A. Deuteronomy 6:4
   Isaiah 43:10
   Isaiah 44:6-8
B. Matthew 28:18-19
   1 Peter 1:2
C. Luke 24:36-53
D. John 1:1-5
   John 1:6-18
E. John 2:18-22

F. John 3:14-17
G. John 3:36
H. John 5:17-18
   John 5:23
I. John 8:56-58
J. John 10:30-38
   Isaiah 7:14
   Matthew 1:18
K. John 14:6-7

L. John 17:2–3
M. John 17:5
N. Acts 1:11
O. Romans 3:23-30
   1 John 1:8-10
P. Romans 6:23
Q. Romans 10:3-10
R. 1 Corinthians 15:1-8
S. 1 Corinthians 15:12-23

T. Ephesians 2:8–9
U. Colossians 1:15-20
V. Colossians 2:9-10
W. 1 Thess. 4:13-18
X. 1 Timothy 2:5–6
Y. 1 Timothy 3:16
Z. Hebrews 1:1-14

How to Become a Christian: The Bible says God loved the world so much that he gave his only begotten Son, that whoever believes in him will not perish but have everlasting life (John 3:16). God loves you and wants a relationship with you. Here are God's promises:
A **All** have sinned and come short of the glory of God (Romans 3:23; 6:23; 1 John 1:10).
B **Believe** on the Lord Jesus Christ, and you will be saved (Acts 16:31, John 1:12).
C If you **Confess** with your mouth the Lord Jesus, and believe in your heart that God raised him from the dead, you will be saved (Romans 10:9; Ephesians 2:8–9).

Biblical Christianity

Founder

Jesus Christ. Founded about AD 30–33, in the Judean province of Palestine (Israel today), under the Roman Empire. Followers of Jesus Christ became known as Christians.

Writings

The Bible, written originally in Hebrew and Aramaic (Old Testament), and Greek (New Testament).

God

The one God is Triune (one God in three Persons, not three gods): Father, Son, and Holy Spirit. Often the title "God" designates the first Person, God the Father. God is a spiritual being without a physical body. He is personal and involved with people. He created the universe out of nothing. He is eternal, changeless, holy, loving, and perfect.

Jesus

Jesus is God, the second Person of the Trinity. As God the Son, he has always existed and was never created. He is fully God and fully man (the two natures joined, not mixed). As the second Person of the Trinity, he is coequal with God the Father and the Holy Spirit. In becoming man, he was begotten through the Holy Spirit and born of the virgin Mary. Jesus is the only way to the Father, salvation, and eternal life. He died on a cross according to God's plan, as full sacrifice and payment for our sins. He rose from the dead on the third day, spiritually and physically immortal. For the next 40 days he was seen by more than 500 eyewitnesses. His wounds were touched and he ate meals. He physically ascended to heaven. Jesus will come again visibly and physically at the end of the world to establish God's kingdom and judge the world.

Holy Spirit

The Holy Spirit is God, the third Person of the Trinity. The Holy Spirit is a person, not a force or energy field. He comforts, grieves, reproves, convicts, guides, teaches, and fills Christians. He is not the Father, nor is he the Son, Jesus Christ.

Salvation

Salvation is by God's grace, not by an individual's good works. Salvation must be received by faith. People must believe in their hearts that Jesus died for their sins and physically rose again, which is the assurance of forgiveness and resurrection of the body. This is God's loving plan to forgive sinful people.

Death

Believers go to be with Jesus. After death, all people await the final Judgment. Both saved and lost people will be resurrected. Those who are saved will live with Jesus in heaven. Those who are lost will suffer the torment of eternal separation from God (hell). Jesus' bodily resurrection guarantees believers that they, too, will be resurrected and receive new immortal bodies.

Other Beliefs

Group worship, usually in churches. No secret rites. Baptism and Lord's Supper (Communion). Active voluntary missionary efforts. Aid to those in need: the poor, widows, orphans, and downtrodden. Christians believe that Jesus is the Jewish Messiah promised to Israel in the Old Testament (Tanakh). Jesus said his followers would be known by their love for one another.

Jehovah's Witnesses
(Watchtower Bible & Tract Society)

Founder	Charles Taze Russell (1852–1916) and later Joseph F. Rutherford (1869–1942). Began 1879 in Pennsylvania. Headquarters in Brooklyn, New York.
Writings	All current Watchtower publications, including the Bible (*New World Translation* only), *Reasoning from the Scriptures*, *You Can Live Forever in Paradise on Earth*. *Watchtower* and *Awake!* magazines.
God	One-person God, called Jehovah. No Trinity. Jesus is the first thing Jehovah created.
Jesus	Jesus is not God. Before he lived on earth, he was Michael the archangel. Jehovah made the universe through him. On earth he was a man who lived a perfect life. After dying on a stake (not a cross), he was resurrected as a spirit; his body was destroyed. Jesus is not coming again; he "returned" invisibly in 1914 in spirit. Very soon, he and the angels will destroy all non-Jehovah's Witnesses.
Holy Spirit	Impersonal "holy spirit" is not God, but rather an invisible, active force from Jehovah.
Salvation	Be baptized as Jehovah's Witnesses. Most followers must earn everlasting life on earth by "door-to-door work." Salvation in heaven is limited to 144,000 "anointed ones." This number is already reached.
Death	The 144,000 live as spirits in heaven. The rest of the righteous, "the great crowd," live on earth, and must obey God perfectly for 1,000 years or be annihilated.
Other Beliefs	Also known as International Bible Students Association (IBSA). Meet in "Kingdom Halls" instead of churches. Active members encouraged to distribute literature door-to-door. Once a year, Lord's Evening Meal (communion); only "anointed" ones may partake. Do not observe holidays or birthdays. Forbidden to vote, salute the flag, work in the military, or accept blood transfusions.

Mormonism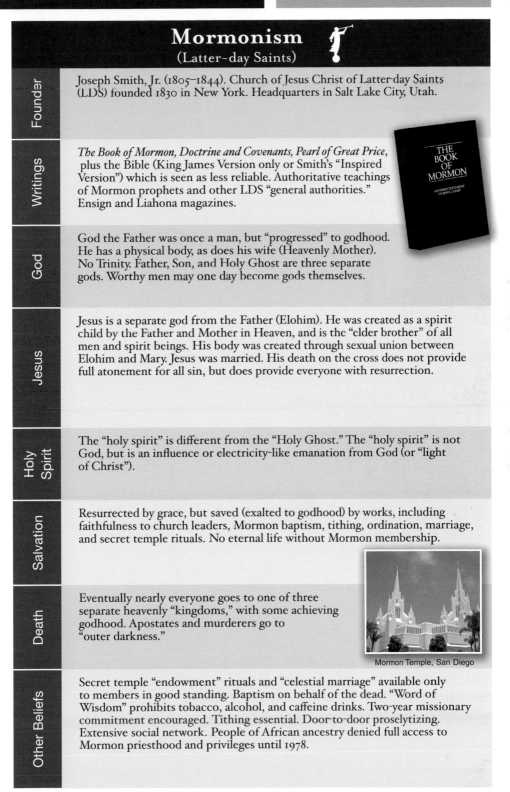
(Latter-day Saints)

Founder

Joseph Smith, Jr. (1805–1844). Church of Jesus Christ of Latter-day Saints (LDS) founded 1830 in New York. Headquarters in Salt Lake City, Utah.

Writings

The Book of Mormon, Doctrine and Covenants, Pearl of Great Price, plus the Bible (King James Version only or Smith's "Inspired Version") which is seen as less reliable. Authoritative teachings of Mormon prophets and other LDS "general authorities." Ensign and Liahona magazines.

THE BOOK OF MORMON
ANOTHER TESTAMENT OF JESUS CHRIST

God

God the Father was once a man, but "progressed" to godhood. He has a physical body, as does his wife (Heavenly Mother). No Trinity. Father, Son, and Holy Ghost are three separate gods. Worthy men may one day become gods themselves.

Jesus

Jesus is a separate god from the Father (Elohim). He was created as a spirit child by the Father and Mother in Heaven, and is the "elder brother" of all men and spirit beings. His body was created through sexual union between Elohim and Mary. Jesus was married. His death on the cross does not provide full atonement for all sin, but does provide everyone with resurrection.

Holy Spirit

The "holy spirit" is different from the "Holy Ghost." The "holy spirit" is not God, but is an influence or electricity-like emanation from God (or "light of Christ").

Salvation

Resurrected by grace, but saved (exalted to godhood) by works, including faithfulness to church leaders, Mormon baptism, tithing, ordination, marriage, and secret temple rituals. No eternal life without Mormon membership.

Death

Eventually nearly everyone goes to one of three separate heavenly "kingdoms," with some achieving godhood. Apostates and murderers go to "outer darkness."

Mormon Temple, San Diego

Other Beliefs

Secret temple "endowment" rituals and "celestial marriage" available only to members in good standing. Baptism on behalf of the dead. "Word of Wisdom" prohibits tobacco, alcohol, and caffeine drinks. Two-year missionary commitment encouraged. Tithing essential. Door-to-door proselytizing. Extensive social network. People of African ancestry denied full access to Mormon priesthood and privileges until 1978.

Unification Church

Founder	Sun Myung Moon (1920–). Started "Holy Spirit Association for the Unification of World Christianity" (Family Federation for World Peace and Unification) in 1954 in Korea. Known in the U.S. as "Lovin' Life Ministries." Based in New York City.
Writings	*Divine Principle* by Sun Myung Moon, considered the "Completed Testament." *Outline of the Principle, Level 4*, and the Bible. (The Bible is "not the truth itself, but a textbook teaching the truth.")
God	God is both positive and negative. God created the universe out of himself; the universe is God's "body." God does not know the future, is suffering, and needs man (Sun Myung Moon) to make him happy. No Trinity.
Jesus	Jesus was a perfect man, not God. He is the son of Zechariah, not born of a virgin. His mission was to unite the Jews behind him, find a perfect bride, and begin a perfect family. The mission failed. Jesus did not resurrect physically. The second coming of Christ is fulfilled in Sun Myung Moon, who is superior to Jesus and will finish Jesus' mission.
Holy Spirit	The Holy Spirit is a feminine spirit who works with Jesus in the spirit world to lead people to Sun Myung Moon.
Salvation	Obedience to and acceptance of the True Parents (Moon and his wife) eliminate sin and result in perfection. Those married by Moon and his wife drink a special holy wine containing 21 ingredients (including the True Parents' blood).
Death	After death one goes to the spirit world. There is no resurrection. Members advance by convincing others to follow Sun Myung Moon. Everyone will be saved, even Satan.
Other Beliefs	Emphasis on mediumism (channeling) to contact the dead, "liberate" souls of one's ancestors. Mass marriages, based on different racial backgrounds, arranged and performed by Moon. Efforts to persuade churches to remove their crosses. Belief that Jesus bows down to Rev. Moon, who is the King of Kings, Lord of Lords, and the Lamb of God.

Essentials of the

UNIFICATION PRINCIPLE

Teachings
of
Sun Myung
Moon

Christian Science

Founder	Mary Baker Eddy (1821–1910). Founded 1875 in Massachusetts. Headquarters in Boston, Massachusetts.
Writings	*Science and Health with Key to the Scriptures, Miscellaneous Writings, Manual of the Mother Church*, and other books by Mrs. Eddy; The Bible (not as reliable); *Christian Science Journal, Christian Science Sentinel*, and other official periodicals.
God	God is an impersonal Principle of life, truth, love, intelligence, and spirit. God is all that truly exists; matter is an illusion.
Jesus	Jesus was not the Christ, but a man who displayed the Christ idea. ("Christ" means perfection, not a person.) Jesus was not God, and God can never become man or flesh. He did not suffer and could not suffer for sins. He did not die on the cross. He was not resurrected physically. He will not literally come back.
Holy Spirit	Holy spirit is defined as the teaching of Christian Science. Impersonal power.
Salvation	Humanity is already eternally saved. Sin, evil, sickness, and death are not real.
Death	Death is not real. Heaven and hell are states of mind. The way to reach heaven is by attaining harmony (oneness with God).
Other Beliefs	Members use Christian Science "practitioners" (authorized professional healers who "treat" supposed illnesses for a fee) instead of doctors. Healing comes through realizing one cannot really be sick or hurt and that the body cannot be ill, suffer pain, or die (matter is an illusion). Attracts followers by claims of miraculous healing. Publishes *Christian Science Monitor* newspaper.

Mary Baker Eddy

Unity School of Christianity   unity

Founder

Charles (1854–1948) and Myrtle (1845–1931) Fillmore. Founded 1889 in Kansas City, Missouri. Headquarters in Unity Village, Missouri.

Writings

Unity magazine, *Lessons in Truth*, *Metaphysical Bible Dictionary*, and the Bible (not as reliable, interpreted with "hidden" meanings).

God

Invisible impersonal power. "God" is interchangeable with "Principle," "Law," "Being," "Mind," "Spirit." God is in everything, much as the soul is in the body. No Trinity. The spirit is reality; matter is not.

Jesus

Jesus was a man and not the Christ. Instead, he was a man who had "Christ Consciousness." "Christ" is a state of perfection in every person. Jesus had lived many times before and was in search of his own salvation. Jesus did not die as a sacrifice for anyone's sins. Jesus did not rise physically and will never return to earth in physical form.

Holy Spirit

The Holy Spirit is the law of God in action, "the executive power of both Father and Son." A "definite" thought in the mind of man.

Salvation

By recognizing that each person is as much a Son of God as Jesus is. There is no evil, no devil, no sin, no poverty, and no old age. A person is reincarnated until he learns these truths and becomes "perfect."

Death

Death is a result of wrong thinking. One moves to a different body (reincarnation) until enlightenment. No literal heaven or hell.

Other Beliefs

Worship services in Unity churches. Counseling and prayer ministry ("Silent Unity") by phone and mail. It is reported that Unity receives millions of prayer requests annually. Unity devotionals, such as *Daily Word*, are used by members of other religious groups and churches. Millions of pieces of literature are printed each year.

Scientology ✝

Founder

Founded by L. Ron Hubbard (1911–1986) in 1954 in California. Major headquarter facilities in California and Florida.

Writings

Dianetics: The Modern Science of Mental Health and others by Hubbard. *The Way to Happiness*.

God

Does not define God or Supreme Being, but rejects biblical descriptions of God. Everyone is a "thetan," an immortal spirit with unlimited powers over its own universe, but not all are aware of this.

Jesus

Jesus is rarely mentioned in Scientology. Jesus was not the Creator, nor was he an "operating thetan" (in control of supernatural powers, cleared from mental defects). Jesus did not die for sins.

Holy Spirit

The Holy Spirit is not part of this belief.

E-Meter Used in "auditing"

Salvation

No sin or need to repent. Salvation is freedom from reincarnation. One must work with an "auditor" on his "engrams" (negative experience units) to achieve the state of "clear." One then progresses up the "bridge to total freedom" to higher "Operating Thetan" states and eventual control over matter, energy, space, and time (MEST).

Death

Hell is a myth, and heaven is a "false dream."

Other Beliefs

Members observe the birth of Hubbard and the anniversary of the publication of *Dianetics*. Controversy follows the group worldwide. *Time* magazine and *Reader's Digest* have published damaging exposés. Organizations related to Scientology include Narconon, Criminon, Way to Happiness Foundation, WISE, Hubbard College of Administration, and Applied Scholastics.

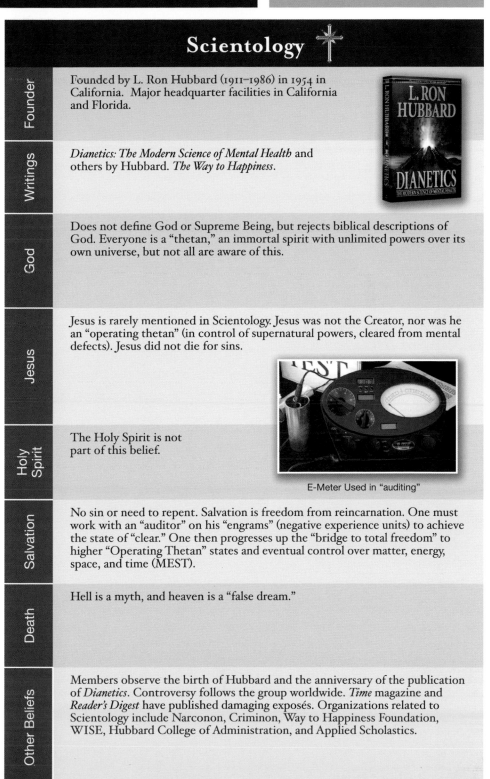

Wicca ⛤

Founder	No one person. Roots in 19th-century Britain. Partly inspired by Margaret Murray (1862–1963) and organized by Gerald Gardner (1884–1964) in the 1930s to 1950s.
Writings	No holy books; however, many groups use *The Book of Shadows*, first compiled by Gardner and later expanded by him and by other leaders. Other popular works include *A Witches' Bible* and *The Spiral Dance*.
God	The supreme being is called the Goddess, sometimes the Goddess and God, or goddess and horned god ("Lord and Lady"). The Goddess can be a symbol, the impersonal force in everything, or a personal being. Wiccans can be pantheists, polytheists, or both.
Jesus	Jesus is either rejected altogether or sometimes considered a spiritual teacher who taught love and compassion.

Objects Used in Divination and Spell-Casting

Holy Spirit	The Holy Spirit is not part of this belief. However, some Wiccans may refer to "Spirit" as a kind of divine energy.
Salvation	Wiccans do not believe that humanity is sinful or needs saving. It is important for Wiccans to honor and work for the preservation of nature (which they equate with the Goddess).
Death	The body replenishes the earth, which is the Goddess's wish. Some Wiccans are agnostic about life after death, others believe in reincarnation. Some believe in a wonderful place called Summerland.
Other Beliefs	Wiccans practice divination and spell-casting, with most rituals performed in a circle. Many Wiccans are part of a coven (local assembly), though many are "solitary." Covens meet for ritual and seasonal holidays, including the eight major holidays (such as Vernal Equinox, Summer Solstice, and Beltane). Wicca is an occultic "nature religion," not Satanism.

New Age

Founder	Based on Eastern mysticism, Hinduism, and paganism. Popularized in part by actress Shirley MacLaine (b. 1934) in the 1980s and 1990s. Beliefs vary.
Writings	No holy book. Use selected Bible passages; I Ching; Hindu, Buddhist, and Taoist writings; and Native American beliefs. Writings on astrology, mysticism, and magic.
God	Everything and everyone is God. God is an impersonal force or principle, not a person. People have unlimited inner power and need to discover it.

Jesus	Jesus is not the one true God. He is not a savior, but a spiritual model and guru, and is now an "ascended master." He was a New Ager who tapped into divine power in the same way that anyone can. Many believe he went east to India or Tibet and learned mystical truths. He did not rise physically, but "rose" into a higher spiritual realm.
Holy Spirit	Sometimes a psychic force. Man is divine and can experience psychic phenomena such as contacting unearthly beings.
Salvation	Need to offset bad karma with good karma. Can tap into supernatural power through meditation, self-awareness, and "spirit guides." Use terms such as "reborn" for this new self-awareness.
Death	Human reincarnations occur until a person reaches oneness with God. No eternal life as a resurrected person. No literal heaven or hell.
Other Beliefs	Can include yoga, meditation, visualization, astrology, channeling, hypnosis, trances, and tarot card readings. Use of crystals to get in harmony with God (Energy) for psychic healing, for contact with spirits, and for developing higher consciousness or other psychic powers. Strive for world unity and peace. Emphasis on holistic health.

Islam

Founder	Founded in Mecca, Arabia by Muhammad (AD 570–632), considered the greatest man who ever lived and the last of more than 124,000 messengers sent by Allah (God). Main types: Sunni ("people of the tradition"), Shi'a ("party of Ali"), Sufi (mystics).
Writings	The Holy Qur'an (Koran), revealed to Muhammad by the angel Gabriel. Essential commentaries are found in the Sunnah ("tradition"), composed of Hadith ("narrative") and Sirah ("journey"). The Qur'an affirms the biblical Torah, Psalms, and Gospels, but Jews and Christians have corrupted the original texts.
God	Allah is One and absolutely unique. He cannot be known. The greatest sin in Islam is shirk, or associating anything with Allah. Human qualities like fatherhood cannot be attributed to Allah. Many Muslims think that Christians believe in three gods and are therefore guilty of shirk.
Jesus	Jesus (Isa in Arabic) was not God or the Son of God. His virgin birth is likened to Adam's creation. He was sinless, a worker of miracles, and one of the most respected prophets sent by Allah. He was not crucified or resurrected. He, not Muhammad, will return to play a special role before the future judgment day, perhaps turning Christians to Islam.
Holy Spirit	"Holy spirit" can refer to Allah, to the angel Gabriel, or to a spirit used by Allah to give life to man and inspire the prophets.
Salvation	Humans are basically good, but fallible and need guidance. The balance between good and bad deeds determines one's destiny in paradise or hell. Allah may tip the balances toward heaven. One should always live with the fear of Allah and judgment day.
Death	Belief in bodily resurrection. One may pray for and seek favor for the dead before judgment day. Paradise includes a garden populated with houris, maidens designed by Allah to provide sexual pleasure to righteous men.
Other Beliefs	Muslims meet in mosques for prayers, sermons, counsel. Emphasis on hospitality, developing a sense of community, and maintaining honor (or avoiding shame). Shari'a (Islamic law) governs all aspects of life in places where it is enforced. Jihad ("fight") may be used to refer either to one's inner struggle to obey God or to literal warfare. Muslims who convert to Christianity or other religions face persecution and possible death.

Nation of Islam

Founder

Wallace D. Fard (1891–?). Founded 1930 in Detroit, but led by Elijah Muhammad (1897–1975) since 1934. Current head is Louis Farrakhan (b. 1933). Headquarters in Chicago, Illinois.

Writings

Publicly, the Holy Qur'an is authoritative and the Bible is quoted often, but *Message to the Blackman in America*, *Our Saviour Has Arrived*, and other books by Elijah Muhammad supply its distinctive views. Current teachings are in *The Final Call* newspaper and speeches of Minister Farrakhan.

God

Officially, there is one God, Allah, as described in the Qur'an. But Elijah Muhammad's teachings are also true: God is a black man, millions of Allahs have lived and died since creation, collectively the black race is God, and Master Fard is the Supreme Allah and Savior.

Jesus

Officially, Jesus is a sinless prophet of Allah. Privately, Jesus was born from adultery between Mary and Joseph, who was already married to another woman. Jesus was not crucified, but stabbed in the heart by a police officer. He is still buried in Jerusalem. Prophecies of Jesus' return refer to Master Fard, Elijah Muhammad, or to Louis Farrakhan.

Elijah Muhammad

Holy Spirit

The Holy Spirit is not significant to their belief, but is generally regarded as the power of God or as the angel Gabriel who spoke to the prophet Muhammad.

Salvation

People sin, but are not born sinful; salvation is through submission to Allah and good works. Older beliefs still held: Fard is the saviour, salvation comes from knowledge of self and realizing that the white race are devils who displaced the black race.

Death

There is no consciousness or any spiritual existence after death. Heaven and hell are symbols. Statements about the resurrection refer to awakening "mentally dead" people by bringing them true teachings.

Other Beliefs

Farrakhan's public messages coexist with earlier, esoteric doctrines. Elijah Muhammad's older views (such as polytheism, God as the black race, Master Fard as Allah incarnate, whites as devils bred to cause harm) are still distributed, but public preaching now focuses on Islamic themes (one eternal God, non-racial emphasis) with frequent use of the Bible.

Bahá'í Faith

Founder	Siyyid 'Alí-Muhammad, "the Báb" (1819–1850) and Mírzá Husayn-'Alí , "Bahá'u'lláh" (1817– 1892). Founded 1844 in Iran. Headquarters in Haifa, Israel.
Writings	Writings of Bahá'u'lláh and 'Abdu'l-Bahá, including *Kitáb-i-Aqdas* ("Most Holy Book") and *Kitáb-i-Íqán* ("Book of Certitude"). The Bible, interpreted spiritually to conform to Bahá'í theology.

Bahá'u'lláh

God	God is an unknowable divine being who has revealed himself through nine "manifestations" (religious leaders), including Adam, Moses, Krishna, Buddha, Jesus, Muhammad, and Bahá'u'lláh. No Trinity.
Jesus	Jesus is one of many manifestations of God. Each manifestation supersedes the previous, giving new teachings about God. Jesus, who superseded Moses, was superseded by Muhammad, and most recently by the greatest, Bahá'u'lláh ("Glory of Allah"). Jesus is not God and did not rise from the dead. He is not the only way to God. The "Christ spirit" returned to earth in Bahá'u'lláh, who is superior to Jesus.
Holy Spirit	Holy Spirit is divine energy from God that empowers every manifestation. "Spirit of Truth" refers to Bahá'u'lláh.
Salvation	Faith in the manifestation of God (Bahá'u'lláh). Knowing and living by Bahá'u'lláh's principles and teachings.

Seat of the Universal House of Justice

Death	Personal immortality based on good works, with rewards for the faithful. Heaven and hell are "allegories for nearness and remoteness from God," not actual places.
Other Beliefs	Bahá'í originated as an Islamic sect and is severely persecuted in Iran. Bahá'í teaches that all religions have the same source, principles, and aims. Stress on oneness and world unity. Regular local gatherings called "feasts," administrative meetings called "spiritual assemblies." "Universal House of Justice" in Haifa, Israel, is the ultimate governing body.

Judaism

Founder	Abraham of the Bible, about 2000 BC, and Moses in the Middle East. There are three main branches of Judaism—Orthodox, Conservative, and Reform—each with its own beliefs.
Writings	The Tanakh (Old Testament), and especially the Torah (first five books of the Bible). The Talmud (explanation of the Tanakh). Teachings of each branch. Writings of sages, such as Maimonides.
God	God is spirit. To Orthodox Jews, God is personal, all-powerful, eternal, and compassionate. To other Jews, God is impersonal, unknowable, and defined in a number of ways. No Trinity.
Jesus	Jesus is seen either as an extremist false messiah or a good but martyred Jewish rabbi (teacher). Many Jews do not consider Jesus at all. Jews (except Messianic Jews and Hebrew Christians) do not believe he was the Messiah, Son of God, or that he rose from the dead. Orthodox Jews believe the Messiah will restore the Jewish kingdom and eventually rule the earth.
Holy Spirit	Some believe the Holy Spirit is another name for God's activity on earth. Others say it is God's love or power.
Salvation	Some Jews believe that prayer, repentance, and obeying the Law are necessary for salvation. Others believe that salvation is the improvement of society.
Death	There will be a physical resurrection. The obedient will live forever with God, and the unrighteous will suffer. Some Jews do not believe in a conscious life after death.
Other Beliefs	Meeting in synagogues on the Sabbath (Sabbath is Friday evening to Saturday evening). Circumcision of males. Many holy days and festivals, including Passover, Sukkoth, Hanukkah, Rosh Hashanah, Yom Kippur, and Purim. Jerusalem is considered the holy city.

Reading of the Torah

Hinduism ॐ

Founder

No one founder. Began 1800–1000 BC in India. Main types: Vaishnavism, Shaivism, and Shaktism.

Writings

Many writings, including
the Vedas (oldest, about 1000 BC),
the Upanishads, and the Bhagavad-Gita.

Vishnu

God

God is "The Absolute," a universal spirit.
Everyone is part of God (Brahman) like
drops in the sea, but most people are not
aware of this. People worship manifestations
of Brahman (gods and goddesses).

Jesus

Jesus Christ is a teacher, a guru, or an avatar
(an incarnation of Vishnu).
He is a son of God as are others.
His death does not atone for sins
and he did not rise from the dead.

Holy Spirit

The Holy Spirit is not part of this belief.

Salvation

Release from the cycles of reincarnation. Achieved through yoga and
meditation. Can take many lifetimes. Final salvation is absorption or union
with Brahman, like a raindrop falling into the ocean.

Death

Reincarnation into a better status (good karma) if a person has behaved
well. If one has been bad, he can be reborn and pay for past sins (bad karma)
by suffering.

Other Beliefs

Many Hindus worship stone and wooden idols in temples, homes. Disciples
meditate on a word, phrase, or picture; may wear orange robes and have
shaved heads. Many use a mark, called a tilak, on the forehead to represent the
spiritual "third eye." Yoga involves meditation, chanting, breathing exercises.
Some gurus demand complete obedience. Foundation of New Age, TM.

Hare Krishna

ISKCON

Founder	AC. Bhaktivedanta Swami Prabhupada (1896–1977) began the International Society for Krishna Consciousness in 1965 in New York. Based on 16th-century Hindu teachings. Headquarters in Mayapur, India.
Writings	*Back to Godhead* magazine. Prabhupada's translations of and commentaries on Hindu scriptures, especially *Bhagavad-Gita As It Is* and *Srimad-Bhagavatam*.
God	God is Lord Krishna. Krishna is a personal creator; the souls of all living things are part of him. ISKCON teaches that what Krishna does freely for his own pleasure (intoxication, sex outside of marriage) is prohibited to his devotees.
Jesus	Jesus is not important to this group. He is usually thought of as an enlightened vegetarian teacher who taught meditation. He is not an incarnation of God. Some Krishna devotees consider Jesus to be Krishna. Others say he is a great avatar (teacher).
Holy Spirit	The Holy Spirit is not part of this belief.
Salvation	Chanting Krishna's name constantly, total devotion to Krishna, worshipping images, and obeying the rules of ISKCON throughout many reincarnated lives releases a follower from bad karma.
Death	Those who are unenlightened continue in endless reincarnation (rebirth on earth) based on the sinful acts of a person's previous life.
Other Beliefs	Public chanting of Hare Krishna "Maha Mantra," yoga, food offerings, soliciting donations. "Four regulative principles" require vegetarian diet, no intoxicants, no gambling, and sex for procreation only. New members are often attracted through feasts and Indian cultural programs. Followers are given new names and may cut family ties.

A.C. Bhaktivedanta Swami Prabhupada

Transcendental Meditation (TM)

Founder	Maharishi Mahesh Yogi (1917–2008). Founded 1955–1958 in India. Based on Hinduism and karma yoga. Headquarters in the Netherlands. Also called World Plan Executive Council.
Writings	Hindu scriptures, including the Bhagavad-Gita, *Meditations of Maharishi Mahesh Yogi*, *Science of Being and the Art of Living*, and other writings by the founder.
God	Each part of creation makes up "God" (Brahman). Supreme Being is not personal. All creation is divine; "all is one."
Jesus	Jesus is not uniquely God. Like all persons, Jesus had a divine essence. Unlike most, he discovered it. Christ didn't suffer and couldn't suffer for people's sins.
Holy Spirit	The Holy Spirit is not part of this belief.
Salvation	Humans have forgotten their inner divinity. Salvation consists of doing good in excess of evil in order to evolve to the highest state (final union of the self with Brahman) through reincarnation.
Death	Reincarnation based on karma (reaping the consequences of one's actions) until loss of self into union with Brahman. No heaven or hell.
Other Beliefs	Mentally recite a mantra (word associated with a Hindu god). Meditate twice a day to relax and achieve union with Brahman. Maharishi University of Management in Iowa offers advanced TM programs in "levitation" and "invisibility." Practices include yoga, Hindu astrology, use of crystals, and idol worship (offerings of flowers, fruit, and cloth for Maharishi's dead teacher, Guru Dev).

His Holiness
MAHARISHI MAHESH YOGI

Science of Being and Art of Living

TRANSCENDENTAL MEDITATION

Buddhism

Founder	Gautama Siddhartha, (563–483 BC), also known as the Buddha ("Enlightened One"). Founded in modern-day Nepal and India as a reformation of Hinduism.
Writings	The Mahavastu ("Great Story," a chaotic collection covering the Buddha's life story), the Jataka Tales (550 stories of the former lives of the Buddha), the Tripitaka ("Three Baskets"), and the Tantras (as recorded in Tibetan Buddhism).
God	The Buddha himself did not believe in the existence of God. Others speak of the Buddha as a universal enlightened consciousness or as a god.

Jesus Christ is not part of the historic Buddhist worldview. Buddhists in the West today generally view Jesus as an enlightened teacher, while Buddhists in Asia believe Jesus is an avatar or a Bodhisattva but not God.

Jesus

Buddha Statue

Holy Spirit

The Holy Spirit is not part of this belief. Buddhists do believe in spirits, and some practice deity yoga and invite spirit possession.

Salvation

The goal of life is nirvana, to eliminate all desires or cravings, and in this way escape suffering. The Eightfold Path is a system to free Buddhists from desiring anything and eventually achieve nonexistence.

Death

Reincarnation. People do not have their own individual souls or spirits, but one's desires and feelings may be reincarnated into another person.

Buddhist Monks

Other Beliefs

Eightfold Path recommends right knowledge, intentions, speech, conduct, livelihood, right effort, mindfulness, and meditation. Some Buddhist groups talk about an "eternal Buddha" (life-force). Through the "Doctrine of Assimilation" the belief systems of other religions are blended into their form of Buddhism.

Soka Gakkai International

Founder

Tsunesaburo Makiguchi (1871–1944) and Josei Toda (1900–1958). Founded 1930 in Japan. Based on 13th-century Nichiren Buddhism. Headquarters in Tokyo, Japan.

Writings

The *Lotus Sutra* (a sutra is a discourse of the Buddha as recorded by his disciples), *The Major Writings of Nichiren Daishonin*, plus writings of Daisaku Ikeda.

God

There is no god in Soka Gakkai. Followers hold to a monistic worldview, believing that there is no separation between creator and creature and that they are protected by Buddhist, Hindu, and Shinto gods that they regard as spiritual forces.

Jesus

Jesus Christ is not part of this belief.

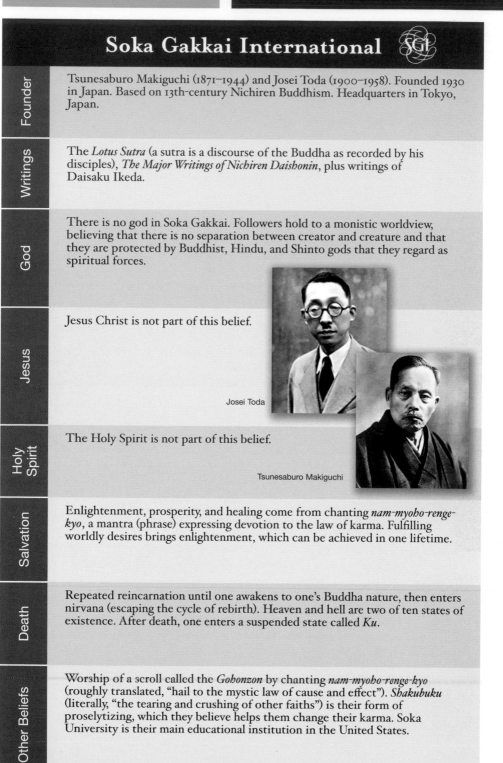

Josei Toda

Holy Spirit

The Holy Spirit is not part of this belief.

Tsunesaburo Makiguchi

Salvation

Enlightenment, prosperity, and healing come from chanting *nam-myoho-renge-kyo*, a mantra (phrase) expressing devotion to the law of karma. Fulfilling worldly desires brings enlightenment, which can be achieved in one lifetime.

Death

Repeated reincarnation until one awakens to one's Buddha nature, then enters nirvana (escaping the cycle of rebirth). Heaven and hell are two of ten states of existence. After death, one enters a suspended state called *Ku*.

Other Beliefs

Worship of a scroll called the *Gohonzon* by chanting *nam-myoho-renge-kyo* (roughly translated, "hail to the mystic law of cause and effect"). *Shakubuku* (literally, "the tearing and crushing of other faiths") is their form of proselytizing, which they believe helps them change their karma. Soka University is their main educational institution in the United States.

Christianity, Cults & the Occult

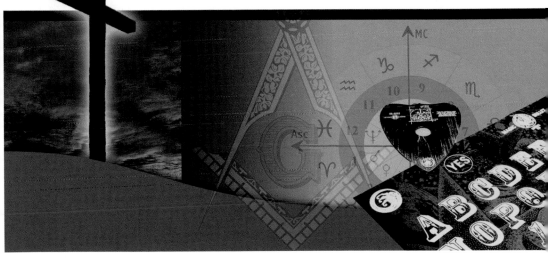

Freemasonry • Kabbalah Centre
Wicca • Satanism • Spiritualism • Santería
Voodoo • Theosophy • Rosicrucianism
Astrology & Horoscopes
Anthroposophy • Eckankar

Biblical Christianity

✛ Origins

Jesus Christ. Founded about AD 30–33 in the Judean province of Palestine (Israel today) under the Roman Empire. Followers of Jesus Christ became known as Christians.

•✦ Key Writings

The Bible, written originally in Hebrew and Aramaic (Old Testament) and Greek (New Testament).

✦ Key Beliefs

The one God is Triune (that is, one God in three Persons, not three gods): Father, Son, and Holy Spirit. Often the title "God" designates the first Person, God the Father. God is a spiritual being without a physical body. He is personal and involved with people. He created the universe out of nothing. He is eternal, changeless, holy, loving, and perfect.

Jesus is God, the second Person of the Trinity. As God the Son, he has always existed and was never created. He is fully God and fully man (the two natures joined, not mixed). As the second Person of the Trinity, He is coequal with God the Father and the Holy Spirit. In becoming man, He was begotten through the Holy Spirit and born of the Virgin Mary. Jesus is the only way to the Father, salvation, and eternal life. He died on a cross according to God's plan, as full sacrifice and payment for our sins. He rose from the dead three days later, spiritually *and* physically immortal. During the next 40 days Jesus was seen by more than 500 eyewitnesses. His wounds were touched and He ate meals. He physically ascended to Heaven. Jesus will come again visibly and physically at the end of the world to establish God's kingdom and judge the world.

The Holy Spirit is God, the third Person of the Trinity. The Holy Spirit is a person, not a force or energy field. He comforts, grieves, reproves, convicts, guides, teaches, and fills Christians. He is not the Father, nor the Son, Jesus Christ.

Salvation is by God's grace, not by an individual's good works. Salvation must be received by faith. People must believe in their hearts that Jesus died for their sins and physically rose again, which is the assurance of forgiveness and resurrection of the body. This is God's loving plan to forgive sinful people.

After death, believers go to be with Jesus. All people await the final Judgment. Both saved and lost people will be resurrected. Those who are saved live with Jesus in heaven. Those who are lost suffer the torment of eternal separation from God (hell). Jesus' bodily resurrection guarantees believers that they, too, will be resurrected and receive new immortal bodies.

Basic teachings are summed up in ancient, universal statements of Christian belief, especially the Apostles' Creed, Nicene Creed, Athanasian Creed, and Definition of Chalcedon.

❖ Key Practices

Include group worship, usually in churches. No secret rites. Baptism and Lord's Supper (communion). Active voluntary missionary efforts. Aid to those in need: the poor, widows, orphans, and downtrodden. Christians believe that Jesus is the Jewish Messiah promised to Israel in the Old Testament (Tanakh). Jesus said his followers would be known by their love for one another.

Freemasonry

✤ Origins

No one founder. Freemasonry Is a secret society which claims descent from the stonemasons of medieval Europe or Solomon's Temple, but which actually started in London in 1717 as a "lodge" with initiations, symbols, and degrees. Masons pass the **Blue Lodge** first and may continue into **Scottish Rite** or **York Rite**. In the U.S.A., the Grand Lodge of each state is the highest authority. Estimated 3.2 million Masons worldwide; about 1.8 million in the U.S.A.

➽ Key Writings

Ceremonies often use a Bible, but may use other "holy books" instead. Popular writings: *The Builders* by Joseph Fort Newton (1914); *Introduction to Freemasonry* by Carl Claudy (1931); *Coil's Masonic Encyclopedia* (1961); and *Mackey's Revised Masonic Encyclopedia* (1966). The Grand Lodge of each state publishes a Monitor of rituals to use (these are similar, but not identical).

✦ Key Beliefs

Masonry claims to transmit secret teachings from ancient times. The "Masonic Edition" of the Bible says, "Masonry is descended from the ancient mysteries." Masonry requires belief in a Supreme Being and treats all religions as though they believe in the same God, whom Masons call by such titles as "Great Architect of the Universe" and "Jah-Bul-On" (supposedly His "secret name").

When the Bible is quoted, references to Jesus are omitted; public prayers must not use Jesus' name. In several rituals Jesus is made equal to Zoroaster, Buddha, or Muhammad. Salvation to the "Grand Lodge above" is achieved by living an upright life, without explicit faith in Christ.

Loyalty binds Masons to one another, and Masons promise by oath of gory death never to reveal their secret rituals to outsiders (curses that are symbolic today). Masonic vows include protection to fellow Masons, even in cases of crime.

▲ Occult Practices

Evangelical researchers John Ankerberg and John Weldon state that Masonry serves as an introduction to the occult because, among other reasons, "in symbolism and philosophy it is similar to many occult practices," and because it is "a system of mysticism which accepts the development of altered states of consciousness." Masonic recommended readings for advanced degrees include works by pagan/occult authors.

👁 Watch for...

- Symbols, such as the **Masonic emblem of "G"** (said to represent God and Geometry) within a **compass** (representing spirituality) and **square** (representing morality).
- Controversies among Christians over whether Freemasonry is truly a religion and whether believers can, in good conscience, be Masons.
- Related institutions: American Masonry historically excluded blacks, so **Prince Hall Masonry** was developed for African-Americans. **Order of the Eastern Star** (for women); **Rainbow Girls** and **Job's Daughters** (for girls); and **DeMolay** (for boys) are "appendant orders." **Shriners** are a separate fraternity for Masons who have completed all the degrees in Scottish or York Rite Masonry.
- Elements derived from Masonry in **Rosicrucianism** and the **Mormon** temple endowment ritual.

Order of the Eastern Star

Rosicrucianism (AMORC)

✛ Origins

H. Spencer Lewis

Said to be founded by **Christian Rosenkreuz** ("rosy cross"), a legendary occultist probably invented in 1614 by **Johann Valentin Andreae** (1586–1654). Europe spawned many Rosicrucian lodges. The largest is the **Ancient Mystical Order Rosae Crucis (AMORC)** — or simply Rosicrucian Order — founded in 1915 by **H. Spencer Lewis** (1883–1939). Headquartered in San Jose, California, AMORC has claimed hundreds of thousands of members in over 100 countries.

➰ Key Writings

Mastery of Life is an introductory booklet. Popular books by Lewis include *The Mystical Life of Jesus* (1929), *The Secret Doctrines of Jesus* (1937), and *Mansions of the Soul* (1930). *Rosicrucian Digest* is published quarterly; *Rosicrucian Forum* is for members only. Inner teachings are disclosed to initiates through secret "monographs" sent by mail, as well as by lectures, directed studies, and members-only gatherings.

✦ Key Beliefs

To AMORC, the Bible is neither unique nor reliable. AMORC literature is openly hostile to Christianity and specifically rejects Christian teachings on God, Christ, salvation, and a host of other key doctrines. Supposedly anyone can use the cult's principles, regardless of church or religion. The advertised goal of life is "mastery of the self." The keys to one's spiritual transformation are buried in many places: Egyptian religions, Hinduism, kabbalah, gnosticism, and Gnostic Christianity. Students use mental techniques to actualize their focused thoughts of health, prosperity, peace, and happiness. Belief in karma, reincarnation, and a "Great White Brotherhood" of highly evolved spiritual masters.

▲ Occultic Practices

AMORC offers a blend of necromancy, mysticism, and Egyptian religion with "development of such psychic powers as telepathy, telekinesis, radiesthesia, clairvoyance, clairaudience, and psychic projection." Occult rituals employ mirrors, incense, candles, herbs, and similar paraphernalia. The AMORC-related Traditional Martinist Order studies kabbalah and engages in ceremonies requiring a black mask.

☽ Watch for…

- Similarities between Masonry and Rosicrucianism: Both run as lodges, initiate members who pass through "degrees," vowing secrecy. Scottish Rite and French Rite Masonry have Rosicrucian degrees. Both present "ancient wisdom," professing the unity of all religions by teaching syncretism. Masonry, Rosicrucianism, and Theosophy influenced one another.
- The tourist-oriented **Rosicrucian Egyptian Museum and Planetarium** in San Jose, California.
- Related groups, such as the **Traditional Martinist Order**; **Rosicrucian Fellowship** of Max Heindel (1865–1919); **Fraternitas Rosae Crucis** of P.B. Randolph (1825–1875); the **Lectorium Rosicrucianum** of Jan Leene, *aka* Jan Van Rijckenborgh (1896–1968); and the **Confraternity of the Rose Cross** of Gary L. Stewart.

Kabbalah Centre

✞ Origins

In broad terms, Kabbalah (from the Hebrew, "to receive") is a form of Jewish mysticism and extrabiblical revelation dating at least to 12th-century Europe. The group now known as **Kabbalah Centre International, Inc.** claims it was founded in 1922 by **Rav Yehuda Ashlag** (1885–1955) in Jerusalem. Others say it was founded in 1969 by Shraga Feivel Gruberger (1927?–), now known as **Philip S. Berg**, who is described as "the world's foremost authority on the Kabbalah." At least 60 locations around the world.

☙ Key Writings

The group's most important text is the *Zohar* ("Book of Splendor"), a 22-volume collection of Hebrew and Aramaic writings and commentaries on the Torah which first appeared in Spain in the 12th or 13th century. Also various books by Philip Berg and his son, Yehuda, including *Kabbalah for the Layman* (1977), *The Essential Zohar* (2002), and *The 72 Names of God: Technology for the Soul* (2003).

✦ Key Beliefs

The Centre's doctrines are radically different from those of orthodox Judaism or Christianity. The supreme being (called *Ein Sof,* "endlessness") is unknowable, infinite, and cannot be named or described. God reveals himself through ten emanations or manifestations, called *sefirot*, which are illustrated with male and female aspects as ten points on the Tree of Life.

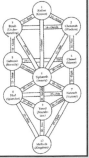

Tree of Life

The 22 letters of the Hebrew alphabet were somehow used to create the world. Humans have a spark of the Creator within. The universe operates on spiritual laws, and Kabbalah enables people to understand and live in harmony with these laws. Man repairs the universe and even God Himself by sharing and living right so that he can hold more of the Creator's light.

He climbs the Tree of Life back to God, and so restores Eden. Ego is a barrier to being like God; we break down ego to become like God. Evil is not a moral issue, but an issue of violating universal principles. Followers believe in reincarnation. The Jewish Messiah is yet to come.

▲ Occultic Practices

The *Zohar* is an encrypted code possessing great mystical power. Meditating on the Hebrew alphabet creates a channel to God; simply scanning the Zohar with one's eyes is sufficient to receive supernatural energy, even if one cannot comprehend what it says. Use of talismans such as a red string bracelet (*bendel*) worn on the left wrist to protect the wearer against the negative spiritual influences of the "evil eye" (described as "a dangerous stream of energy that emanates from the eyes of another person"). Use of other items said to possess spiritual power, such as Kabbalah Water (with special healing properties), magical stones, scented candles, incense, and eye cream. Extensive use of astrology and meditation. Philip Berg is said to possess miraculous spiritual powers.

Title page of the Zohar, 1558

◉ Watch for...

- Controversies over expensive merchandise, courses, and fundraising methods.
- Widespread opposition by mainstream Jewish leaders, who denounce the Centre as a deceptive cult.
- Famous followers are said to include entertainers Madonna, Demi Moore, Elizabeth Taylor, and Britney Spears.
- Related institutions include **Spirituality for Kids** (educational program) and **Oroz Research Centre** (develops products with supernatural powers).
- Red string bracelets.

Wicca

✥ Origins

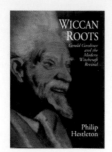

No one founder. Wicca has its roots in 19th-century Britain. It was partly inspired by **Margaret Murray** (1862–1963) and founded by **Gerald Gardner** (1884–1964) in 1939. Some Wiccans believe it to be the oldest religion. Wicca is a subset of Neopaganism, which a revival of ancient polytheism and reverence for the forces of nature. In both, nature is the model. Wicca sometimes focuses more on the Goddess and has different rituals from other pagan practices.

◀✦ Key Writings

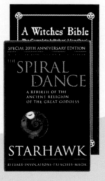

No holy books; however, many groups use *The Book of Shadows*, first compiled by Gardner and later expanded by him and by other leaders. Other popular works include *The Spiral Dance* by Starhawk (1979) and *A Witches' Bible* by Janet and Stewart Farrar (1996).

✦ Key Beliefs

Wiccans can be pantheists, polytheists, or both. The supreme being is called the Goddess, sometimes the Goddess and God, or goddess and horned god ("Lord and Lady"). The Goddess can be a symbol, the impersonal force in everything, or a personal being. Jesus is either rejected altogether or sometimes considered a spiritual teacher who taught love and compassion. Wiccans do not believe that humanity is sinful or needs saving.

It is important for Wiccans to honor and work for the preservation of nature (which they equate with the Goddess). At death one's body replenishes the earth, which is the Goddess's wish. Wiccans generally state no specific belief about life after death, though some believe in reincarnation and others believe in going to a wonderful place called Summerland.

▲ Occultic Practices

Wiccans practice divination and spell-casting, with most rituals performed in a circle. Many Wiccans are part of a coven (local assembly), though many are "solitary." Covens meet for ritual and seasonal holidays, including the 8 major holidays (such as Vernal Equinox, Summer Solstice, and Beltane). Wicca is an occultic "nature religion," not Satanism.

◉ Watch for...

- Increasing popularity of books and products related to various kinds of witchcraft, paganism, and Goddess-worship. These include do-it-yourself spell-casting kits, candles, incense, lotions, and jewelry — often targeting young adult consumers.
- Wicca-themed web sites and chatrooms for adults and teenagers.
- Pop-culture versions of witches and witchcraft, as seen in mainstream films (like *Practical Magic* and *The Craft*), television programs (like *Charmed*, *Sabrina the Teenage Witch*, and *Buffy the Vampire Slayer*), and fiction (such as *Teen Witch* and *Wild Girls: The Path of the Young Goddess*).
- Increasing acceptance of organized groups, such as pagan student unions on college and university campuses.
- Controversies over Wiccans serving as chaplains in prisons, hospitals, and the military.

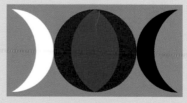

Wiccan Triple Moon Symbol

The Church of Satan/Satanism

✦ Origins

First Church of Satan was founded by **Anton Szandor LaVey** (1930–1997) in San Francisco, California, in 1966. Many Satanic groups have modeled themselves on the Church of Satan.

✦ Key Writings

The Satanic Bible (1969), *The Satanic Witch* (1971), and other works by LaVey.

✦ Key Beliefs

Satanism thoroughly and forcefully rejects biblical Christian doctrine and ethics and is man-centered in the extreme. God is viewed as an impersonal balancing force of nature; LaVey writes that those who believe in a literal God invented him as an externalized form of their own ego. Jesus is regarded as either mythical or a failure. While some Satanists believe that Satan is a real, personal being, those who follow LaVey's teachings usually do not. Instead, Satan symbolizes man as his own god and opposition to all religions. Man is just another animal and should be free of moral codes. Belief in sin is designed to make men feel guilty so that they can be controlled by hypocritical religious systems. Though man should learn from his mistakes, there is no need for salvation. There is no life beyond death; life is to be lived now, vitally and pleasurably.

There are "Nine Satanic Statements," or principles, some of which are: Man should indulge, not abstain; be kind only to the deserving; and take vengeance instead of turning the other cheek ("Do unto others as they do unto you"). Satanists look down on those who want to do good, calling them "white-lighters."

▲ Occultic Practices

Satanic magic is based primarily on desire, manipulation, imagery, and force of will done in ritual. For the Satanist, there is no such thing as "black or white magick"; there is only magic. LaVey wrote that "Satanic Ritual is a blend of Gnostic, Cabbalistic, Hermetic, and Masonic elements" employing "vibratory words of power." Some Satanists perform a blasphemous ceremony known as the "black mass." The most important holidays are the Satanist's own birthday; April 30th (climax of spring equinox), and October 31st.

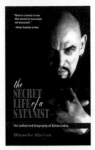

👁 Watch for...

- Related groups, including the **Temple of Set**, founded in 1975 by **Michael Aquino**. Formal Satanist organizations have generally been short-lived. Many individuals are self-styled Satanists, improvising beliefs and rituals.
- Reports of satanist-inspired crime. Sensationalistic accounts of vast conspiracies of child-murdering Satanists have consistently been debunked.
- Popular films, novels, and rock bands have used Satanist-inspired imagery for shock value.
- Famous followers, said to include entertainers Jayne Mansfield, Sammy Davis Jr., and Marilyn Manson. Convicted multiple murderer Richard Ramirez (the "Night Stalker") was reportedly a Satanist.

Spiritualism

✝ Origins

No one founder. This ancient belief was widely popularized in the United States in 1848 by sisters **Margaret Fox** (1838–1893) and **Kate Fox** (1841–1892) of Hydesville, New York.

Margaret Fox

Kate Fox

➪ Key Writings

Include *Spiritualist Manual* (1911); *Aquarian Gospel of Jesus the Christ* by Levi H. Dowling (1908); *Oahspe* by John Ballou Newbrough (1882); and the Bible (selected portions).

✦ Key Beliefs

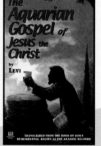

Despite their clear denial of central biblical teachings, many spiritualists believe themselves to be practicing an early, authentic form of Christianity. God is seen as an impersonal power controlling the universe. Jesus was a man, not God incarnate. While on earth, he was a prophet or an advanced medium (one believed to communicate with the spirit world). Jesus is now a spirit with whom one can communicate in the spirit world.

Some use the term "holy spirit" to refer to the spirit of a holy person who once lived. After life on this earthly plane, life continues in the spirit world, where one's spirit may progress from one level to the next. Heaven and hell are considered states of mind. Some spiritualists believe in reincarnation and karma.

▲ Occultic Practices

Mediums conduct séances to contact the dead, assorted psychic demonstrations. Church services feature singing, music, sermons, spirit messages from the dead, and prophecies. Spiritualists may use Ouija™ boards, crystal balls, and other instruments of divination. Spiritualism often attracts grieving people who hope for contact with a deceased loved one.

◉ Watch for...

- The **National Spiritualist Association of Churches**, representing over 100 churches; there are many other small groups, but no single central spiritualist organization.
- The symbol of the **sunflower**, regarded as "the emblem of spiritualism" ("As the sunflower turns its face to the light of the sun, so Spiritualism turns the face of humanity to the light of truth").
- "Spiritism" as a system of beliefs codified by French author Hippolyte Léon Denizard Rivail (1804–1869), *aka* **Allan Kardec**. Kardecism has millions of followers in Latin America.
- Newspaper articles about spiritualist communities in Lily Dale, New York and Cassadaga, Florida.
- Famous followers, including Sir Arthur Conan Doyle (1859–1930), creator of the Sherlock Holmes detective series.

Ouija® board with planchette

Santería

✢ Origins

No one founder. Santería (from the Spanish, "way of the saints") — also called *lucumí* and *Regla de Ocha* — comes primarily from the religion of the Yoruba people of southwestern Nigeria, who were brought to Cuba in the 16th–19th century as slaves. Santería was mainly brought to the U.S.A. by Cubans fleeing Fidel Castro's regime.

☙ Key Writings

None. Santería's beliefs and practices are based primarily on oral traditions and vary from place to place. Some of the most authoritative written descriptions are Spanish-language works by Cuban author Lydia Cabrera, especially *El Monte* (1954).

El Monte
LYDIA CABRERA

Letras Cubanas

✦ Key Beliefs

Santería is an animistic religion but has many Roman Catholic followers. Santería acknowledges a remote creator god, called *Olofi* or *Olodumare*. Followers must placate a variety of capricious spirits, including dozens of lesser deities (*orishas*) and spirits of the dead (including ancestors, slaves, Indians, and gypsies). Orishas are associated with forces of nature and with Roman Catholic saints (*santos*). The main orishas are known as the *Siete Potencias Africanas* (seven African powers), each having its own elaborate mythology. Jesus is considered to have been "a great sorcerer." *Ashé* is considered a neutral cosmic energy. Santería teaches reincarnation.

▲ Occultic Practices

Santería has been described as "jungle magic adapted to city living." Diviners use cowrie shells, coconuts, and other sacred objects to identify and solve personal problems. Spirit possession occurs frequently in group rituals, which can also include animal blood sacrifices (mostly chickens and goats) and the use of various herbs and plants. Use of sacred stones (*otanes*) and various talismans thought to possess great spiritual power.

◎ Watch for...

- "Botánicas," shops in mostly Latino neighborhoods where statues, candles, bones, roots, and other Santería products are sold.
- Remains of animal sacrifices and offerings left on street corners for the spirits.
- Simple clay images (with eyes, nose and mouth made of cowrie shells) representing the messenger/trickster orisha Eleggúa.
- **Abakuá** and **Palo Monte/Palo Mayombe** are related movements emphasizing black magic. Other related movements include **macumba**, **Umbanda**, and **candomblé** (Brazil); and **voodoo** (Haiti).
- Famous followers, said to include entertainers Desi Arnaz, Celia Cruz, and Mongo Santamaria.
- In the U.S.A., Santería is spreading most quickly in areas with large numbers of Latino immigrants, such as Miami, New York, Chicago, and Los Angeles.

Santería priestess

Eleggúa

Voodoo

✚ Origins

No one founder. Voodoo — also spelled *vodou* (from the Fon *vodu*, "spirit" or "deity") was brought by West African slaves to colonial Haiti, where it is now the dominant religion. It first entered the United States after the Haitian revolt of 1804.

●✚ Key Writings

None. Voodoo's beliefs and practices are based primarily on oral traditions and vary from place to place.

✦ Key Beliefs

A vèvè, symbol representing a lwa

Haitian voodoo is an animistic religion and combines many elements of African cults, Roman Catholic imagery and ritual, and even European folklore. There are two main types voodoo: *Rada* (seen by practitioners as benign) and *Petro* (seen as dominated by black magic). Voodoo acknowledges a remote creator god, called *Bondye*. Humans must deal with three main types of spirits: *lemistè* (also known as *loa* or *lwa*), *lemó* (the dead), and *lemarasa* (the sacred twins). There are thousands of the capricious lwa, among the most important of which are *Ezili* (associated with Our Lady of Mt. Carmel, love, and beauty) and *Dambala* (associated with St. Patrick and snakes). After death, one part of man's spirit goes to Bondye, and another goes to *Gine* (a kind of African spiritual homeland); there is also a belief in reincarnation.

▲ Occultic Practices

Spirits, summoned ritually by drums, are said to "mount" (possess) worshippers like horses, speaking and acting through them. Various kinds of divination and sorcery are used for protection, healing, direction, luck, and inflicting harm on enemies. Ritual offerings — including food, drink, and animal sacrifices — are made to appease the spirits. Cemeteries are important to some rituals.

👁 Watch for...

- Voodoo should not be confused with **hoodoo**, a form of folk magic originating in the southern U.S.A. (though the two have some things in common).
- Sensationalized "zombies" (the walking dead) and "voodoo dolls," as shown in some novels and movies, that do not reflect main voodoo beliefs.
- Related movements, including **Santería** (Cuba) and **Tambor de Mina** (Brazil).
- In North America, voodoo is most common in areas with Haitian immigrant communities, such as Miami, New York City, Montreal, and Chicago. New Orleans, Louisiana, has its own peculiar form of voodoo.

Theosophy

✥ Origins

Theosophy (from Greek *theosophos*, "one wise about God" or "divine wisdom") is an esoteric philosophy and movement tracing its modern origin to **Helena P. Blavatsky**

(1831–1891), also known as "Madame Blavatsky" or HPB. In 1875 she founded the **Theosophical Society** in New York with **Henry Steel Olcott** (1832–1907). Four years later,

Helena P. Blavatsky the Society moved to India where it grew quickly, eventually becoming the fountainhead of the "ancient wisdom" doctrine within Western occultism.

●✦ Key Writings

Blavatsky's *The Secret Doctrine* (1888), *Isis Unveiled* (1877), and *The Key to Theosophy* (1889). Periodicals include *Sunrise*.

✦ Key Beliefs

"Ancient wisdom" teachings hold that the world's religions (Greek, Egyptian, Christian, gnostic, Buddhist, etc.) originally taught the same core truths, but were corrupted by the development of organized religion. The oldest scriptures (the Hindu *Vedas*) contain the kernel truths and the others carry parts of this core: monism, reincarnation, yoga, evolution of consciousness, psychic powers, etc.

Invisible to us, the evolutionary progress of Earth has been directed for thousands of years by a seven-tiered hierarchy of Masters or superior beings. Some were originally human, died, and are now "Ascended Masters" (also known as the "Great White Brotherhood"); others are still alive; some never had human embodiment. The Masters reveal themselves to a few select souls, either in remote parts of the world (China, Tibet) or through psychic communication, giving guidance to those who are prepared for it. Blavatsky claimed communication with several of these so-called Masters, as did most of her immediate successors.

Jesus is considered the fifth incarnation in the Aryan race of the Christ, or supreme "World Teacher." Theosophy rejects Jesus' atonement and states that man brings about his own salvation through repeated incarnations; every human being is a potential "Christ."

▲ Occultic Practices

Yoga and meditation are employed in spiritual development; psychic powers (including "easy access" to the mystic "Akashic Records"), astral travel, and other paranormal abilities may follow, depending on the individual. Astrology and some other occult practices are considered "true sciences." An inner circle, known as the "Esoteric Section," engages in secret meditation practices to attune its members with the Masters.

◉ Watch for…

- Related theosophical institutions, including the **Theosophical Society** (Altadena, California); **Theosophical Society in America** (Wheaton, Illinois), with its **Krotona School** and **Quest Books**; and the **United Lodge of Theosophists** (Pasadena, California).
- Famous followers, such as children's authors L. Frank Baum (*The Wizard of Oz*) and Frances Hodgson Burnett (*The Secret Garden*), and poet W.B. Yeats.
- Theosophy-inspired groups, such as the **Krishnamurti Foundations**, based on the teachings of Jiddu Krishnamurti (1895–1986); the **Arcane School** of Alice Bailey (1880–1949); **Anthroposophy**; the **Agni Yoga Society** of Nicholas Roerich (1874–1947); the **"I AM" movement**; and the **Church Universal and Triumphant** of Elizabeth Clare Prophet (1939–2009).

Anthroposophy

✛ Origins

Anthroposophical Society was founded in Germany in 1912 by Austrian psychic **Rudolf Steiner** (1861–1925) as a breakaway group from Theosophy. World headquarters located at the Goetheanum in Dornach, Switzerland.

Rudolf Steiner

↩ Key Writings

All of Steiner's works are considered authoritative. This includes some 6,000 lectures, hundreds of essays, and 33 books, including *A Philosophy of Freedom* (1894), *Christianity as Mystical Fact* (1902), and *An Outline of Occult Science* (1910).

✦ Key Beliefs

Steiner claimed to receive information directly from the spiritual realm. Anthroposophy is based on his personal revelations, which describe an extremely complex evolutionary history for mankind. He began as a believer in Theosophy and embraced such Theosophical concepts as karma and reincarnation. Anthroposophy is relentlessly man-centered and pays little attention to traditional questions about "God" or our relationship to Him.

Though Steiner called his system "true Christianity," he also called it "Christian Occultism" and radically redefined Christian terms. Steiner saw the Bible not as revelation "from without," but as a picture of human potential. He describes two separate "Jesuses" who merged spiritually, after which a "Christ-occence" entered and remained for three years. At the crucifixion, Jesus' blood did not redeem us from sin, but flowed into the physical earth, where its mystical power energizes our cosmic evolution and frees us from the bonds of materialism. This enables the Christ-essence to "mass-incarnate" into the whole of humanity (which is the true "second coming").

▲ Occultic Practices

The central tenet of Anthroposophy is that humans have an ability to contact the spiritual realm directly which can be awakened through exercises in concentration and meditation. The practice of Anthroposophy consists mostly of such exercises. Like all forms of occult meditation, this can open the door to intrusions from the unseen world, including spirit contact and associated phenomena, such as clairvoyance, divination, and mediumship. Astral projection and astrology are also important components of Anthroposophy.

The Anthroposophical Society in America

☾ Watch for…

- Controversy over Steiner-oriented **Waldorf Schools**, with parents claiming they were not made aware of the profoundly occultic basis of its educational system when their children enrolled.

- Anthroposophy-inspired organizations, such as **Weleda** (personal and healthcare products); **curative eurythmy** (therapeutic dance); **bio-dynamic farming** (organic agriculture with magical/occult elements); **Camphill Movement** (communities for disabled/special-needs people); **The Christian Community** (a Steiner-oriented church); and the **Christian Occult Society** (name used by some local Steiner groups).

- Famous followers, such as writer and philosopher Owen Barfield and influential New Age author David Spangler.

Eckankar

✣ Origins

Founded in San Diego, California by **Paul Twitchell** (1908–1971) in 1965. Proclaims itself the "Religion of the Light and Sound of God" and "the Ancient Science of Soul Travel." Current headquarters in Chanhassen, Minnesota.

➬ Key Writings

The Shariyat-Ki-Sugmad (1970) — considered "sacred scripture" — and other books by Paul Twitchell, including *The Tiger's Fang* (1967), *Eckankar: The Key to Secret Worlds* (1969), and *The Flute of God* (1970); writings by Sri Harold Klemp, the current "Living Eck Master."

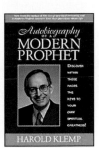

Autobiography of a MODERN PROPHET — Discover within these pages the keys to your own spiritual greatness!

HAROLD KLEMP

✦ Key Beliefs

God is a formless essence consisting of light and sound, called the *Sugmad* (said to be "neither masculine nor feminine" and "the source of all life"). The light and sound flow out of the Sugmad and return to it in a current called the *Eck.* Christianity is acknowledged as "an alternate path" to "a degree of enlightenment." The biblical concept of the Trinity is not recognized by Eckankar. Twitchell taught that the Devil "is the Jehovah of the Jewish faith and the Father of the Christian teachings.... Therefore we really see Jesus as a son of Kal Niranjan...." — that is, the Devil. (Elsewhere the group teaches that Jesus was "the ECK Master in Judea.") "Holy Spirit" is used as another name for the "Eck" current. Enlightenment, or union with the Sugmad, is attained by tuning in to the Eck current through "soul travel" and following it as it returns to its source. After death one is reincarnated, repeatedly, until one returns to the Sugmad.

▲ Occultic Practices

Eckankar's practice is based on "soul travel," which is similar to an "out-of-body" experience. This is said to be "taught only by the Living ECK Master" and made possible by more than 100 "spiritual exercises," such as visualization and chanting "HU" ("The most ancient, secret name for God"). While "soul-travelling" one can meet with dead Eck Masters and follow the Eck current back to the Sugmad. Members, called *chelas*, pass through a series of initiations, the first of which "often comes in a dream."

◉ Watch for...

- Related groups, including **Church of the Movement of Spiritual Inner Awareness** (MSIA) and **Insight Seminars**, founded by John-Roger Hinkins (1934–); Ford Johnson's **Higher Consciousness Society**; and Gary Olsen's **MasterPath**.
- The **Temple of Eck**, a 50,000-square foot building at the group's Chanhassen, Minnesota, headquarters, regarded as "the keystone of the teachings of ECK on earth."
- Longstanding controversies, including charges that Twitchell plagiarized much of his writing and most of his teaching from **Kirpal Singh** (1894–1974), a Radhasoami guru he had once followed (but later denied knowing), and from Scientology, which he had also followed.

An Inspiring Guidebook on How to Follow the Call of God

THE FLUTE OF GOD

Paul Twitchell

Astrology and Horoscopes

✛ What Are They?

Astrology (from the Greek *astrología*, "telling of the stars") — A form of divination that interprets the positions of the sun, moon, and planets as meaningful representations of a person's life, of an event, or of any entity that has a founding date (such as a country). Astrology differs from *astronomy*, which is the scientific study of space and heavenly bodies.

Horoscope (from the Greek *horoskópos*, "time observer") — Newspaper horoscope columns are based primarily on the interpretation of the positions of the faster-moving moon and closer planets as influences on the twelve zodiac sun signs. (Professional astrologers often dismiss horoscopes because only the sun sign is taken into consideration.)

Zodiac (from the Greek *zóion*, "animal") — An imaginary belt in the heavens divided by astrologers into twelve equal divisions, or "signs." The three main types of astrology practiced today are *western* (originating in the Middle East), *Vedic* (from India), and *Chinese*, each with its own theories and very different zodiac signs.

▲ What Do Astrologers Do?

Natal astrology — Planetary positions at birth are seen as the blueprint for a person's life, including past, present and future. The chart is read to assess family, social, relationship, career, and spiritual factors and potentials in the person's life. The astrologer synthesizes planetary signs, positions, the 12 houses, and other factors in the chart. The positions of the planets as they move around the birth chart indicate future influences and trends. Relationship charts are fashioned by making a composite of two charts, or by comparing two or more charts.

Mundane astrology — Chart for an event, city or country. The event could be an earthquake, political election, declaration of war, or any event with a timed beginning.

Horary astrology — Chart done to answer a question. The astrologer notes the time of the question and interprets the resulting chart in order to answer the question.

☽ What Makes Astrology Appealing?

In his book *Wisdom from India: Astrology*, Christian apologist Vishal Mangalwadi identifies four key reasons why astrology "thrives in such troubled times":

- It offers an explanation for our troubles
- It removes a sense of guilt and responsibility
- It offers hope
- It offers guidance when people feel hopeless

✖ What Makes Astrology "Work"?

Astrology is not merely forbidden in the Bible—it's demonic. Charles Strohmer, a former professional astrologer, writes in his book *What Your Horoscope Doesn't Tell You:* "As we look honestly at astrology, we begin to see that adherents of this system — without knowing it — are banging on the door through which communication is established with knowledgeable but yet deceptive spirit beings." He further explains that the horoscopic chart is used by the astrologer as the mediumistic point of interaction, and that "without contact with spirit beings, there would be no astrological self-disclosures."

▶ What Does the Bible Say about Astrology?

Since it is a form of divination, astrology is forbidden in passages like Leviticus 19:26 ("Do not practice divination or sorcery"). We also gain insight from such verses as

- Isaiah 47:13–15 — *"Astrologers" and "stargazers" mocked and condemned.*
- Jeremiah 8:1–2; 10:2 — *Those who follow, worship, consult the sun, moon, and stars condemned.*
- Daniel chapters 2, 4, 5 — *After astrologers and other diviners declare that interpreting Nebuchadnezzar's dreams and Belshazzar's vision is "impossible," Daniel does so with God's help.*

Terms and Definitions

ASTRAL PROJECTION, ASTRAL TRAVEL: The ability to travel outside one's body during sleep or while in a trance state.

CHANNELING: Allowing a spirit (demon) to speak through you; also called mediumism.

DEGREE: A stage of advancement or attainment.

DEMON: A fallen angel who serves Satan. Can impersonate dead persons (such as ghosts) and other spirit beings.

DIVINATION: Reading hidden meanings in natural objects and/or receiving information about one's past, present, or future through supernatural means. Examples: astrology; numerology (*arithmancy*); reading cards (*cartomancy*), palms (*chiromancy*), glass or still water surfaces such as a crystal, mirror, or lake (*scrying*), tea leaves (*tasseomancy*), hexagram patterns (*I Ching*) or special Norse symbols (*runes*), and the earth to determine the best location for structures (*geomancy*).

FAMILIAR SPIRIT: A spirit that aids in divination or magic; demon.

LODGE: Can be used to refer to a governing body, branch, meeting hall, or members of an organization (e.g., Freemasons, Theosophists, Rosicrucians).

MAGIC(K): To bend reality to one's will by using supernatural or mysterious powers. (Not to be confused with stage magic practiced by illusionists for entertainment.)

MEDIUM: Psychic who attempts to communicate with the dead and/or other spirit beings.

NECROMANCY: A form of divination in which one seeks to communicate with the spirits of the dead. (From the Greek *nekrós*, "corpse," and *manteía*, "divination.") May also be used to refer to witchcraft or black magic in general.

OCCULT: Practices to uncover hidden meanings or use supernatural powers, or contact with spirits. The English word "occult" comes from the Latin *occulere*, "to conceal."

OUIJA® BOARD: Popular "talking board," a device manufactured by Parker Bros. and widely used in necromancy and divination. Often promoted as a fun children's game, Ouija boards can be a "doorway to the occult."

POSSESSION: Being inhabited and controlled by a demon.

PSYCHIC: Someone who gains information through paranormal powers of seeing (*clairvoyance*) or hearing (*clairaudience*).

REINCARNATION: The rebirth of a soul in another body. This may occur over many lifetimes until the soul has evolved enough to attain a more perfect state.

SATAN: Powerful angel who rebelled against God and tempts and deceives man.

SORCERY: The use of drugs or spirits to access supernatural power; sometimes considered by occultists to be the use of harmful or black magic.

SPELL: Verbal formula believed to possess supernatural power.

SPIRIT: A being with no physical body, such as an angel or demon.

SPIRITISM: Attempting to contact a disembodied being such as a dead person or an angel.

SPIRIT GUIDE: A disembodied entity who acts as one's guide; a demon.

SUPERNATURAL: Above or beyond what is natural; abnormal or extraordinary.

SYNCRETISM: The fusion of different systems of belief.

TALISMAN, AMULET: An object or set of secret words or symbols with supernatural power.

TAROT: A set of 78 illustrated cards used for divination.

WITCHCRAFT: The practice of occult arts; also, a modern religion based on the belief that nature is divine, and belief in the Goddess or many gods. Modern witchcraft religion, which includes a category called Wicca, is a subset of Neopaganism, a revival of ancient pagan polytheism and magical practices.

NOTE: Not all occultists agree on how these terms should be defined. Some who engage in the practices believe that their powers are merely natural, not supernatural. This comparison chart is not intended to arouse an unhealthy curiosity about hidden and forbidden things; instead, it is meant to help discern danger so you can avoid it, resist it, and help others.

Scriptural Warnings on the Occult

In both the Old and New Testaments, God commands His people to abstain from occult practices of any kind — in the strongest possible terms. Scripture consistently associates occult activity with superstition, idolatry, deception, fear, futility, uncleanness, and rebellion. God regards such things as evil, demonic, and deserving of swift and severe judgment.

NOTE: In the Bible, some of the same Hebrew and Greek terms can be translated into English as *witchcraft, sorcery, enchantments, divination,* and *soothsaying,* depending on different Bible versions.

THE BIBLE CONDEMNS MAGIC ARTS, ENCHANTMENTS
Genesis 41:8, 24
Exodus 7:11, 22; 8:7; 18–19
Leviticus 19:26
Deuteronomy 18:10
2 Kings 17:17; 21:6
2 Chronicles 33:6
Isaiah 47:9, 12
Jeremiah 27:9
Acts 8:9–11; 18–21; 13:6–12; 19:19
Revelation 9:20, 21; 18:23; 21:8; 22:15

THE BIBLE CONDEMNS THE USE OF MAGICAL CHARMS, AMULETS
Isaiah 3:18–20
Ezekiel 13:18–20

THE BIBLE CONDEMNS SORCERY
Exodus 22:18
Leviticus 19:26
Deuteronomy 18:10, 14
2 Kings 17:17; 21:6
2 Chronicles 33:6
Isaiah 47:9
Jeremiah 27:9–10
Micah 5:12

Nahum 3:4
Acts 8:9–11; 19:19
Galatians 5:19–21
Revelation 9:21; 18:23; 21:8; 22:15

THE BIBLE CONDEMNS SPIRITISM, THE CONSULTING OF MEDIUMS, AND NECROMANCY (ATTEMPTING TO CONTACT THE DEAD)
Leviticus 19:31; 20:6
Deuteronomy 18:10–11
1 Samuel 28:3, 9
2 Kings 21:6; 23:24
1 Chronicles 10:13
2 Chronicles 33:6
Isaiah 8:19; 19:3
Jeremiah 27:9

THE BIBLE CONDEMNS CASTING SPELLS
Deuteronomy 18:9–11
Isaiah 47:9, 12
Micah 5:12

THE BIBLE CONDEMNS DIVINATION
Leviticus 19:26
Deuteronomy 18:10, 14
1 Samuel 15:23
2 Kings 17:17; 21:6
2 Chronicles 33:6
Isaiah 2:6
Jeremiah 27:9–10
Acts 16:16–20

THE BIBLE CONDEMNS WITCHCRAFT (REFERRING NOT TO A SPECIFIC RELIGION, BUT TO OCCULT PRACTICES GENERALLY)
Deuteronomy 18:10, 14
1 Samuel 15:23
2 Kings 21:6
2 Chronicles 33:6
Micah 5:12
Nahum 3:3–4
Galatians 5:19–21

Why Choose These Groups?
The occult takes many forms. Often occultism is practiced and promoted through organized groups—some of them admittedly religious, some not. Some of the movements described here (like Theosophy) may seem small, but their influence far exceeds their membership. Freemasonry itself has few occultic elements, but its rituals have been adapted by many occultic groups. Other religious groups with occultic roots (such as Mormonism and Scientology) are not listed here; the main focus is on groups openly practicing occultism today.

General Editor: Paul Carden – Executive Director, The Centers for Apologetics Research
Contributors: Brooks Alexander, Marcia Montenegro, Eric Pement, Marcelo Souza.

Christianity
& Eastern
Religions

Hinduism
Vaishnavism • Shaivism • Shaktism

Buddhism
Theravada • Mahayana • Vajrayana

Sikhism • Confucianism • Taoism • Shinto

Christianity
& Eastern
Religions

THE GROWTH OF EASTERN RELIGIONS
AND WHAT IT MEANS TO CHRISTIANS

A century ago the average westerner knew little to nothing about East Asian religions like Buddhism and Hinduism. But with rapid changes in travel and technology, eastern worldviews and practices have gained enormous influence in western culture. For example, in 1900 an estimated 1% of Americans believed in reincarnation, compared with roughly 25% of the U.S. population today. With missionary zeal, Hindu gurus and Buddhist monks—such as the Maharishi Mahesh Yogi (Transcendental Meditation) and the Dalai Lama (Tibetan Buddhism)—have traveled throughout the West to promote their religions. Simultaneously, eastern philosophies have gained many followers, influenced by yoga, feng shui, martial arts, macrobiotic diets, acupuncture, and ayurvedic therapies.

BELIEFS OF EASTERN RELIGIONS

There are important differences in the major eastern religions, and not all scholars agree on points of history and classification. Still, many foundational beliefs of eastern belief systems stand in stark contrast to the Christian worldview. To see how Christianity and eastern religions differ, it's helpful to understand basic concepts common to most eastern religions and New Age thought:

Pantheism is a bedrock of eastern religious philosophy. The meaning of the word comes from the Greek *pan* ("all") and *theos* ("God"). In pantheism, God is not separate from creation. "God" in pantheism is not a personal, loving, creator as in Christianity, but a vague, impersonal force that exists in all things. Although some eastern religions incorporate devotion to gods or spirit beings, they generally reject belief in an all-powerful, loving, personal God with whom anyone can have a personal relationship.

Reincarnation is a foundational belief in eastern religions, in which souls go through thousands of births, lives, and deaths. Karma—the spiritual principle of cause and effect—is the negative agent that causes people to reincarnate. In early Hindu scriptures, reincarnation is described as smoke from a cremated soul rising into the clouds, where it falls back to the earth as rain that nourishes plants and animals in the food chain, eventually becoming human again. This is the opposite of the Christian belief that God creates us as individuals with one physical life on earth—in which we can accept or reject his loving gift of salvation—followed by a single resurrection.

Yoga and meditation are two of the main ways of attaining "salvation" in eastern religions. Salvation means escaping the countless painful cycles of reincarnation. Yoga and meditation are physical and mental practices developed as ways of reducing one's karma—the attachment to the physical world and our individual selves. In Christianity, salvation is the free gift from God through his love and grace to anyone who will accept it; in eastern religions, salvation is something people constantly work to achieve by their own efforts.

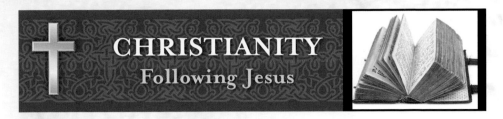

CHRISTIANITY
Following Jesus

▶▶▶ ORIGINS
Founded c. AD 30 in the Judean province of Palestine (modern Israel) under the Roman Empire.

▶▶▶ FOUNDER
Jesus Christ (c. 4 BC–AD 33). Adherents known as Christians.

▶▶▶ OTHER MAJOR HISTORICAL FIGURES
• **Moses** (c. 15th-13th century BC)
• **Paul the Apostle** (1st century AD)

▶▶▶ MAJOR SACRED WRITINGS
▶ The **Holy Bible**, divided into the Old Testament, 39 books written mainly in Hebrew and Aramaic; and New Testament, 27 books written in Greek.

▶▶▶ KEY BELIEFS
God: The one God is triune (One God in three Persons, not three gods): Father, Son and Holy Spirit. Often the title "God" refers to the first person, God the Father. God is a spiritual being without a physical body. He is personal and involved with people. He created the universe out of nothing. He is eternal, changeless, holy, loving and perfect. Jesus is God, the second Person of the Trinity. As God the Son, he has always existed and was never created. He is fully God and fully man (the two natures are joined, not mixed). As the second Person of the Trinity, he is coequal with God the Father and the Holy Spirit. In becoming man, he was begotten through the Holy Spirit and born of the Virgin Mary. Jesus is the only way to the Father, salvation and eternal life. The Holy Spirit is God, the Third Person of the Trinity. The Holy Spirit is a *person*, not a force or an energy field. He comforts, grieves, reproves, convicts, guides, teaches and fills Christians. He is not the Father, nor the Son, Jesus Christ.

Purpose of Life/Salvation: Salvation is by God's grace, not an individual's good works. Salvation must be received by faith. People must believe in their hearts that Jesus died for their sins and physically rose again, which is the assurance of forgiveness and resurrection of the body. This is God's loving plan to forgive sinful people. After death, believers go to be with Jesus. All people await the Final Judgment. Both saved and lost people will be resurrected. Those who are saved will live with Jesus in Heaven. Those who are lost suffer eternal separation from God (Hell). Jesus' bodily resurrection guarantees believers that they too will be resurrected and receive new immortal bodies.

Other Beliefs: Jesus is the Jewish Messiah promised to Israel in the Old Testament. Basic teachings are summarized in the ancient statements of Christian belief, especially the Apostles' Creed, the Nicene Creed, the Athanasian Creed, and the Definition of Chalcedon.

▶▶▶ DISTINCTIVE PRACTICES
Group worship, usually in churches, but no secret rites. Baptism and communion (Lord's Supper) are central. Active missionary efforts, aid to those in need (poor, widows, orphans, the downtrodden).

▶▶▶ MAJOR CELEBRATIONS
• **Easter**, commemorating Jesus' resurrection (annual; dates vary)
• **Christmas**, commemorating Jesus' birth (annual; December 25)

▶▶▶ MAJOR DENOMINATIONS
• *Roman Catholicism* and *Eastern Orthodoxy* separated in AD 1054 (the Great Schism).
• *Protestantism* separated from Roman Catholicism in AD 1517 (the Reformation).

▶▶▶ ADHERENTS/DISTRIBUTION
Worldwide: an estimated 2 billion professing Christians, concentrated in the Americas, Europe, and Africa.

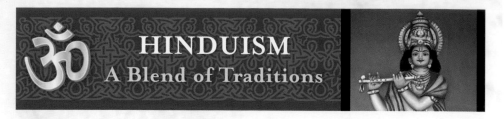

HINDUISM
A Blend of Traditions

▶▶▶ ORIGINS
North India, c. 1500 BC. Hindu scholars from India often try to trace its roots to the Indus River civilization (c. 3000 BC), but this ancient culture lies in present-day Pakistan and had more in common with ancient Mesopotamia than with Hindu India.

▶▶▶ FOUNDER
None. Hinduism has no single founder and no single unifying philosophy or tradition. It evolved as a mingling of historic religious influences that are not necessarily compatible with one another.

▶▶▶ MAJOR HISTORICAL FIGURES
• **Adi Shankara** (AD 788–820), considered the greatest philosopher of Hinduism; refined earlier pantheism into a philosophy known as *Advaita Vedanta* (or Monism) in which God is totally impersonal and without attributes.
• The **Alvar saints** of south India (c. AD 800–1000), among the most important founders of the Bhakti (devotional) schools of Hinduism, worshiping God as a supreme person or one or more of the manifestations of God (such as Rama or Krishna). This philosophy was the opposite of Shankara's impersonal Monism, and is reflected today in the Hare Krishna movement.

▶▶▶ MAJOR SACRED WRITINGS
There are hundreds of Hindu scriptures. The most important collections are:
▶ the four **Vedas** ("knowledge") (c. 1500–1000 BC), the earliest texts
▶ the **Brahmanas** (c. 900–500 BC), consisting mainly of rituals and mantras
▶ the **Upanishads** (c. 800–500 BC), 108 philosophical treatises
▶ the **Dharmashastras** (c. 100 BC–AD 200), ethical, civil, and criminal law (including the **Laws of Manu**)
▶ the **Brahma Sutras** (c. AD 100), 550 verses of cryptic descriptions on God, reality, salvation, and other matters
▶ the **Ramayana** (c. 500 BC) and the **Mahabharata** (c. 400 BC—AD 300), epic poems (the latter including the **Bhagavad Gita**)
▶ the **Puranas** (c. AD 400–1000), containing the "history of the universe"
▶ the **Tantras** (c. AD 300–1100), containing magical/occult rituals and spiritual exercises to accelerate enlightenment

▶▶▶ KEY BELIEFS
God: Originally a religion of many gods (*polytheism*), Hinduism gradually developed into a philosophy known as *pantheism* (all is God), which teaches that the Divine is in everything and that everything is divine. Theistic and pantheistic views of God are taught by different schools of Hindu thought, and are often mingled. In the non-theistic traditions, God is *not* a personal creator, distinct from his creation, but both the creature and its source are part of the same "big reality," called *Brahman-Atman.* Brahman is the Divine Totality, the ultimate reality, and Atman is the individual soul, like a spark from the huge fire of Brahman. As the 20th century Indian guru Muktananda said, "Worship your own inner self. God lives within you as you."

There are said to be as many as 33 million gods in Hinduism, and most Hindus worship god(s) in spite of philosophical speculations about worshiping self. Shiva and Vishnu are monotheistic deities in some of the theistic Hindu traditions. Other popular deities include Kali/Durga/Shakti, Krishna, Rama, Ganesh, and Hanuman.

Purpose of Life/Salvation: Each human soul is destined to eventually merge with Brahman through thousands of reincarnations and much suffering. These life cycles, called *samsara* ("wandering"), refer to the soul's journey from one life to another until achieving *moksha* ("liberation"). In the non-theistic traditions, this liberation is nothing like "heaven." One's final release from suffering and the cycles of reincarnation occurs when the soul dissolves into Brahman (the Universe), like a raindrop falling into the ocean. Moksha amounts to the extinction of the individual personality; but in the theistic traditions there is a concept of heaven as being present with God. Unlike Judaism and Christianity, Hinduism views history in terms of vast cycles of creation and destruction, including four eras known as *yugas*; this understanding permeates its doctrines and practices.

▶▶▶ DISTINCTIVE PRACTICES

In India, upper-caste Brahmin priests preside over rituals and ceremonies invoking various gods; these rituals may serve both religious and cultural purposes. Hindus meditate repeating the same words and phrases (*mantras*) and use many images for worship. *Puja* (worship) includes food, flower, and incense offerings accompanied by prayers and mantras. Advanced spiritual seekers become disciples of *gurus,* some of whom claim high spiritual attainment even to the point that they will not be reincarnated because they have attained "enlightenment." "Guru and God are one" is a common expression. The guru and his disciple have a relationship that is intimate and complex, creating a psychological and spiritual bond. During the disciple's initiation the guru whispers a secret mantra into the disciple's ear, and the disciple may even surrender his will and personality to the guru.

▶▶▶ MAJOR CELEBRATIONS
- **Kumbh Mela** ("festival of the pot")— a triennial pilgrimage, rotating among four locations in India; the world's largest religious gathering
- **Diwali**—an annual festival of lights (October or November)

▶▶▶ MAJOR DENOMINATIONS
- ***Shaivism***—a tradition with multiple expressions, the most significant one (Shaiva Siddhanta) being theistic rather than impersonalistic
- ***Vaishnavism***—emphasizes the worship of Vishnu, understands Brahman in terms of more personal manifestations (such as Ram and Krishna, hero of the Bhagavad Gita)
- ***Shaktism***—emphasizes devotion to Shakti or the Devi (the divine mother) as the ultimate expression of the godhead

▶▶▶ ADHERENTS/DISTRIBUTION
Estimated 1 billion worldwide. Majority in India (making up 80% of the population); significant following in Nepal, Indonesia (Bali), South Africa, the Caribbean.

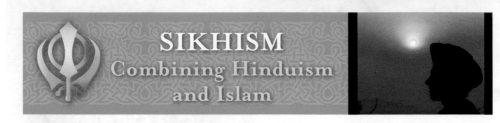

SIKHISM
Combining Hinduism and Islam

▶▶▶ ORIGINS
Late 15th century AD in what is now the Punjab state of northern India.

▶▶▶ FOUNDER
Guru Nanak (AD 1470–1540) received a vision to preach the true way to enlightenment and God. Nanak combined Islamic monotheism and Hindu reincarnation, while rejecting idol worship and the oppressive Indian caste system. He also appropriated elements of Sufism (the mystical branch of Islam).

▶▶▶ MAJOR SACRED WRITINGS
▶ The **Sri Guru Granth Sahib** (or Adi Granth), first compiled in AD 1604, contains nearly 6,000 *shabads* (hymns), composed in nine languages, by the first nine Sikh gurus and various Hindu and Muslim saints. It is worshiped by Sikhs and regarded as their 11th and perpetual guru.
Other holy books include:
▶ the **Dasam Granth**, a varied compilation of writings
▶ the **Varan Bhai Gurdas**, a commentary
▶ the **Rahatnamas**, codes of conduct
▶ the **Sau Sakhi**, a compilation of prophecies

▶▶▶ KEY BELIEFS
God: Nanak believed in one omnipresent God known only by those spiritually awakened through meditation. Sikhism is also pantheistic, considering the universe itself to be a part of God, leaving no clear distinction between the Creator and his creation.

Purpose of Life/Salvation: Bondage to the material realm and the "five evils"—ego, anger, greed, attachment, and lust—condemn the soul to numerous reincarnations. Those who are successful in overcoming these evils through proper behavior and devotion will be released from reincarnation and achieve union with God.

▶▶▶ MAJOR DENOMINATIONS
Distinction is made between **Khalsa** (full, baptized) Sikhs and **Sahadjari** (not fully observant) Sikhs. Other subgroups:
• *Radha Soami*—Indian sect formed in 1861; influenced 20th-century Western occult groups such as **Eckankar** and **MSIA** (Movement for Spiritual Inner Awareness)
• *Healthy, Happy, Holy* (*3HO*)—Sikh-inspired movement led by Harbhajan Singh Yogi, better known as Yogi Bhajan (1929–2004)

▶▶▶ DISTINCTIVE PRACTICES
The Golden Temple (or *Harmandir Sahib*) of Amritsar is the main center of worship; there are also numerous local/individual worship centers (*gurdwaras*). Followers are expected to recite scripture after rising and bathing in the morning. Sikhs are forbidden to cut their hair; adult males are identifiable by their use of a turban (*pagri* or *dastar*). Sometimes Sikhs wearing turbans have been mistaken for Muslims.

▶▶▶ ADHERENTS/DISTRIBUTION
Estimated 23 million, mainly in the Punjab region of northern India.

HINDUISM
IN THE WEST

The increasing interest in Hindu ideas in North America can be traced partly through the controversial careers of well-known gurus, including:

Maharishi Mahesh Yogi (1917–2008)
- Founded the Transcendental Meditation (TM) movement in India in 1957 (as the Spiritual Regeneration Movement)
- Emphasized a "mechanical" path to enlightenment
- Gained early popularity through his association with the Beatles, the Beach Boys, and other entertainers in the 1960s
- Suffered a major setback when U.S. federal courts ruled that his meditation technique and "Science of Creative Intelligence" were religious, despite his claims to the contrary

A.C. Bhaktivedanta Swami Prabhubada (1896–1977)
- Founded the International Society for Krishna Consciousness (ISKCON)—or "Hare Krishna"—movement in New York in 1966
- Emphasized *bhakti yoga* and Vaishnavism
- Followers became known for their saffron robes, dancing on city streets, and aggressive fundraising techniques

Sathya Sai Baba (1926?–)
- Leader of the International Sai Organization, based in Puttaparthy, India
- Claims to be God
- Famous for his purported miracles, alleged by some to be hoaxes

Swami Muktananda Paramahansa (1908–1982)
- Founded the SYDA Foundation (also known as Siddha Yoga) in 1974
- Claimed to be God
- Emphasized *kundalini yoga* (also called *maha yoga*)

Paramahansa Yogananda (1893–1952)
- Founded the Self-Realization Fellowship in 1920
- Emphasized *kriya yoga*
- Most famous for his book *Autobiography of a Yogi* (1946)

Osho, also known as **Bhagwan Shree Rajneesh** (1931–1990)
- Emphasized *tantra yoga* and enlightenment through sexual techniques
- Famous for his ability to transmit spiritual energy to his devotees

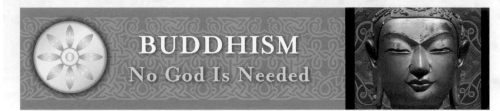

BUDDHISM
No God Is Needed

▶▶▶ **ORIGINS**
Southern Nepal, c. 5th century BC

▶▶▶ **FOUNDER**
Siddhartha Gautama (563–483 BC), now known as Buddha ("awakened one"). Siddhartha was born into a ruling clan, and led a life of ease in which he was protected from all knowledge of human misery. When he subsequently encountered an old man, a sick man, and a decaying corpse, the shock sent him into a search to find a solution to life's suffering. He went on a pilgrimage of inquiry and meditation, but grew frustrated with the Hindu teachers he found. One day while sitting under a Bodhi tree in northern India, he suddenly experienced "enlightenment" or "awakening," realizing that souls have the illusion of being reincarnated and floating through eternity, bound in ignorance, and suffering senselessly in one body after another.

▶▶▶ **OTHER MAJOR HISTORICAL FIGURES**
• **Ashoka** (273–232 BC), Indian emperor who was the first to enthusiastically spread Buddhism by sending missionaries as far as the Mediterranean
• **Nagarjuna** (c. AD 150–250), Indian philosopher and founder of the Madhyamaka school; considered the most influential Buddhist after the Buddha himself

▶▶▶ **MAJOR SACRED WRITINGS**
The oldest and most authoritative scriptures are the massive Pali Canon, or **Tripitaka** ("three baskets"), an oral tradition of the life and sayings of Buddha committed to writing some 500 years *after* his death. It can be divided into three main collections:
▶ the **Vinaya Pitaka** ("basket of discipline"), a code of ethics for monks and nuns
▶ the **Sutra Pitaka** ("basket of threads"), accounts of the Buddha's teachings
▶ the **Abhidharma Pitaka** ("basket of scholasticism"), philosophical works

▶▶▶ **KEY BELIEFS**
God: Often considered a kind of "atheistic religion." Central to Buddha's teachings is the idea that pursuing or knowing "God" is irrelevant and can even impede one's quest for enlightenment. Buddha considered the Hindu gods as beings who are under the power of karma and who need to become human, convert to Buddhism, and achieve spiritual awakening. (Still, in Buddhist literature the idea of a monotheistic creator God is often mentioned and rejected.) Buddha considered it his mission to guide souls through the web of suffering and ignorance into salvation (*nirvana*). He called the source of creation "dependent origination"—the source of suffering, existence, and all problems.

Purpose of Life/Salvation: Buddha's awakening under the Bodhi tree caused him to immediately begin preaching his teaching, known as the *Dharma*—the underlying order and truth of existence. Buddhism's fundamental principle may be summed up in the phrase "All is suffering" (*Sabbham dukkham*). Buddha taught that there are "Four Noble Truths," namely:

1. **The reality of suffering**
2. **The cause of suffering** (craving/desire)
3. **The cessation of suffering** (nirvana)
4. **The "middle way"—following the Eightfold Noble Path** (Right Understanding, Right Thoughts, Right Speech, Right Action, Right Livelihood, Right Endeavor, Right Mindfulness, Right Concentration)

As in Hinduism, salvation depends on meditation, austerities, and becoming a monk. Traditionally, only male monks can attain salvation—the release from the painful cycle of reincarnation. Salvation is called *nirvana* (literally "blown out," like a candle flame that vanishes). Nirvana resembles the atheist's concept of death—the annihilation of personal existence. This state of nonexistence is also called the *sunya* ("great void"), which is empty of all things.

▶▶▶ DISTINCTIVE PRACTICES

Some Mahayana Buddhist schools venerate enlightened spirits through demonstrations of respect, meditation, and gift giving. The five *silas* of moral conduct require Buddhists to refrain from killing, theft, sexual misconduct, lying or evil speech, and using illicit drugs and liquor. Zen Buddhism rejects theoretical knowledge and sacred writings in favor of experiencing sudden enlightenment through intensive seated meditation, often meditating on illogical anecdotes and word puzzles (such as, "What is the sound of one hand clapping?") under the direct guidance of a Zen practitioner.

▶▶▶ MAJOR CELEBRATIONS

- **Uposatha**, four monthly holy days
- **Vesak**, an annual commemoration of Buddha's birthday (May/June)
- **Vassa**, an annual rainy-season retreat (July–October)
- **Ullambana** (All Souls Day), emphasizing veneration of ancestors (August)

▶▶▶ MAJOR DIVISIONS/DENOMINATIONS

- **Theravada** ("path of the elders," also called *Hinayana*, or "lesser vehicle")—emphasizes *Samadhi* ("concentration") meditation and *Vipassana* ("insight") meditation. Strongly affirms the existence of the historical Buddha ("Sakyamuni").
- **Mahayana** ("greater vehicle")—stresses that the essential Buddha-nature can be attained by all persons through meditation and the aid of *bodhisattvas*—enlightened beings who return to earth to aid Buddhists in spiritual need.
- **Vajrayana** ("diamond vehicle"), popularized by the Dalai Lama—combines Mahayana, Indian Tantra, and the occultic Bön religion of ancient Tibet (which promotes the worship of dark spirits). **Shingon** Buddhism in Japan is derived from Vajrayana.

▶▶▶ ADHERENTS/DISTRIBUTION

Approximately 350 million, largely concentrated in East Asia. The world's fourth-largest religion.

THE DALAI LAMA
Widely Known, Little-Understood Spiritual Celebrity

Tenzin Gyatso (1935–), the 14th **Dalai Lama** ("ocean of wisdom"), was born in rural Tibet. A monk of the *Gelug* ("Yellow Hat") sect of Tibetan Buddhism, he is said to be the reincarnation of the previous thirteen Dalai Lamas, the god-kings of Tibet (considered manifestations of *Avalokitesvara*, bodhisattva of compassion). In 1959, he fled Tibet because of conflict with the ruling Chinese, and now heads the Tibetan government in exile in Dharamsala, India. The Dalai Lama has done far more than anyone else to popularize Tibetan Buddhism in the West, cultivating well-publicized friendships with celebrities.

But there is more to the story. In 2001 the Dalai Lama told an interviewer for *Christianity Today* that "Jesus Christ also lived previous lives," adding that Jesus "reached a high state, either as a Bodhisattva, or an enlightened person, through Buddhist practice or something like that." Researcher James Stephens notes that Tibetan Buddhism uses "a rigorous system of works righteousness" to enable followers to accumulate sufficient merit to "achieve deliverance from the ... cycle of rebirths. These works include reciting mantras and sutras, ...deity yoga, utilizing Buddhist rosary beads, prayer wheels, prayer flags and mani stones, visualizing demonic entities, and making symbolic offerings." Few people realize that the Dalai Lama's religion is also deeply occultic, thanks in part to the influence of the ancient Bön religion. The Dalai Lama consults the spirit-possessed Nechung Oracle for state decisions, and the Tantrism of Tibetan Buddhism includes the ritual use of human remains and of bodily excretions known as the "five ambrosias."

CONFUCIANISM
The Foundation of Chinese Religion

▶▶▶ ORIGINS
China, 6th century BC.

▶▶▶ FOUNDER
Confucius or Kong Zi (551–479 BC), perhaps the most revered and influential figure in Chinese history.

▶▶▶ OTHER MAJOR HISTORICAL FIGURES
• **Meng Zi** or Mencius (372–289 BC), philosopher and author who emphasized striving for the common good
• **Xun Zi** (c. 300–230 BC), philosopher who emphasized the evil of human nature and the need for ritual and authority

▶▶▶ MAJOR SACRED WRITINGS
The "Four Books" of the Confucian canon are:
▶ The **Analects of Confucius** (c. 479–221 BC), compiled by his disciples shortly after his death
▶ The **Great Learning**, attributed to Confucius and Zengzi (505–436 BC)
▶ The **Doctrine of the Mean** by Zisi (481–402 BC)
▶ The **Book of Mencius**, attributed to the author of the same name
Other important writings include:
▶ The **Book of Filial Piety** (c. 400 BC)
▶ The "Five Classics," a collection which includes the **Classic of Changes** or **I Ching** (c. 1150 BC), a system of divination

▶▶▶ KEY BELIEFS
God: Not everyone considers Confucianism an actual religion, and Confucius did not speak of God or gods. Despite this, he and nearly 200 disciples and sages are now worshiped in Confucian temples.

Purpose of Life/Salvation: While he did uphold the Chinese concept of "Heaven" as an overarching spiritual reality, Confucius was a humanist concerned with ethical behavior in government and interpersonal relations. His ideal was the harmony of the perfected individual within a well-ordered society. His teachings can be summed up as "ethical humanism." He taught that the truly superior man is motivated by righteousness instead of profit. Confucius did not speak of an afterlife or the soul, but he condoned the ancient Chinese practice of ancestor worship—but more as an ethical system of respect for the dead.

Other Beliefs: Include an emphasis on cultivating "filial piety" (a love and respect for one's parents and ancestors) and adhering to the laws of nature.

▶▶▶ DISTINCTIVE PRACTICES
Rituals include offerings to the spirits of ancestors, as well as observances to mark important stages of life (such as births, weddings, and funerals).

▶▶▶ MAJOR CELEBRATIONS
• **Teacher's Day**, observed annually in Taiwan in honor of Confucius' birthday (August 27)
• **International Confucius Cultural Festival** in Confucius' birthplace in Qufu, China (September–October)

▶▶▶ MAJOR DIVISIONS/ DENOMINATIONS
A "New Confucian" movement began in the 20th century, reflecting the Neo-Confucian movement of AD 960–1279 that reveres Confucius, Buddha, and Laozi.

▶▶▶ ADHERENTS/DISTRIBUTION
An estimated 300 million Chinese consider themselves Confucians. Besides mainland China, Confucianism has had a significant influence on the cultures of Taiwan, Japan, Korea, and Vietnam.

TAOISM (DAOISM)
Going with the Flow

▶▶▶ ORIGINS
Tao ("the way") began in China in the 6th century BC, reaching near-final form by the 2nd century BC. Adopted as a state religion by AD 440.

▶▶▶ FOUNDER
Laozi ("the old man"), also called Lao-Tzu (c. 600–530 BC), said to be a contemporary of Confucius (though his true identity and historicity are in doubt). His most famous saying is, "The journey of a thousand miles begins with the first step."

▶▶▶ OTHER MAJOR HISTORICAL FIGURES
Zhuangzi (370–301 BC), Laozi's noted disciple, popularized the Tao, defining it as the spiritual process of constant flow or give-and-take.

▶▶▶ MAJOR SACRED WRITINGS
▶ **Tao Te Ching**, ascribed to Laozi
▶ **Zhuangzi**, ascribed to the author of the same name
▶ The much larger compilation of all Taoist works is the **Daozang** ("Treasury of Tao"), collected around AD 400

▶▶▶ KEY BELIEFS
God: Taoism is polytheistic, with worship of deities such as the Jade Emperor. Laozi himself came to be venerated as a deity, along with many other "immortals."

Purpose of Life/Salvation: Taoism's doctrines vary widely, and include numerous naturalistic or mystical Asian beliefs. "Tao" refers to the way that life flows on both spiritual and material planes. It is the force behind the natural order, or the principle that keeps the universe balanced and ordered. *Yin* is passive, weak and disorganized, while *Yang* is active, strong and integrative. The Yin and Yang can be harmonized through meditations and practices called *Wu wei* ("not doing"). The goal of Wu wei is alignment with Tao, revealing the smooth, invisible power within all things. Salvation is a vague concept in Taoism. Some Taoists believe in reincarnation, while others believe life after death is a continuation of life on earth upheld by ancestor worship.

Other Beliefs: Include an emphasis on "five precepts" of interpersonal ethics, much like the five *silas* of Buddhism.

▶▶▶ DISTINCTIVE PRACTICES
Occult practices include spirit possession, mediumship, and divination (employing the *I Ching*, astrology, or Feng Shui—a form of geomancy that interprets geographic shapes and features, and arranges objects to attract "good energy"). Taoism has also influenced Chinese martial arts (such as *Tai chi chuan*), traditional medicine, and *qigong*.

▶▶▶ MAJOR CELEBRATIONS
• **Qingming Festival**—in which food offerings are made to deities and the spirits of the dead (annual, early April)

▶▶▶ MAJOR DIVISIONS/DENOMINATIONS
• *Tianshi Dao* ("Way of the Celestial Masters")
• *Zhengyi Dao* ("Way of Orthodox Oneness")
• *Quanzhen* ("Complete Perfection")
• *Shangqing* ("Supreme Clarity")
• *Lingbao* ("Sacred Jewel")

▶▶▶ ADHERENTS/DISTRIBUTION
Estimated at 200 million worldwide, mostly in China, although influence continues to grow steadily in North America.

SHINTO
Japan's Native Religion

▶▶▶ ORIGINS
From the Chinese *shin tao* ("the way of the gods"). Native Japanese animist religion dating to 500 BC or earlier.

▶▶▶ FOUNDER
None. Shinto creation legends tell of native deities, called *kami,* who formed the islands of Japan.

▶▶▶ MAJOR SACRED WRITINGS
Numerous texts dating from the 8th century AD and later. The four of the most important texts are:
▶ the **Kojiki** (AD 712), and **Nihon Shoki** (AD 720), two of Japan's national epics
▶ the **Rikkokushi** ("six national histories"), which includes
  • the **Shoku Nihongi** (AD 697–791)
  • the **Jinno Shotoki** (AD 1338–1341), a treatise on Japanese politics and history

▶▶▶ KEY BELIEFS
God: God is regarded not as personal creator, but as the force behind all the *kami* spirits. All of nature is animated by the kami—including things such as rocks, trees, or streams—making Shinto a combination of polytheism and pantheism. There are more than a dozen major kami, including *Ameratasu,* the sun goddess (represented in the rising sun of Japan's national flag), from whom the emperors of Japan descended.

Purpose of Life/Salvation: The main purpose of human existence is to lead an ethical life. After death each person continues existence as a kami.

Other Beliefs: Japan's current emperor, Akihito (son of Hirohito, who ruled during World War II), is still regarded as divine by some Japanese.

▶▶▶ DISTINCTIVE PRACTICES
The kami are worshiped in Japan's many shrines presided over by Shinto priests. Each shrine is dedicated to a specific kami who is said to respond to sincere prayers of the faithful. Prayers to the kami are offered for all of life's difficulties and blessings. Shinto recognizes many sacred places: mountains, springs, and significant historical locations.

▶▶▶ MAJOR CELEBRATIONS
Shinto is fundamental to the numerous *Matsuri* (festivals) held in Japan throughout the year.

▶▶▶ MAJOR DIVISIONS/DENOMINATIONS
There are more than two dozen distinct Shinto schools.

▶▶▶ ADHERENTS/DISTRIBUTION
About 85% of Japan's population of 127 million embraces both Shinto and Buddhism. Nearly all followers are Japanese; very few non-Japanese convert. Shinto has influenced many of the so-called "new religions" exported from Japan to the Americas and Western Europe, including **Mahikari**, **Perfect Liberty Kyodan**, **Church of World Messianity**, and **Seicho-No-Ie**.

BUDDHISM
IN THE WEST

Significant Buddhist movements in North America and Western Europe include:

Zen (Ch'an)
- Imported from China and established as a separate school in Japan in the 12th century
- Emphasizes sudden and spontaneous enlightenment (*satori*)—the experience of one's true nature
- Main schools: Soto, Rinzai, and Obaku

Soka Gakkai International
- 20th-century Japanese sect based on the teachings of Nichiren Daishonin (AD 1222–1282)
- Emphasizes chanting of the "Lotus Sutra" (*nam-myoho-renge-kyo*) before a divine scroll (*Gohonzon*) to obtain what one wants
- Claims 15 million members in 190 countries

Nichiren Daishonin

Shambhala International (Vajradhatu) and Naropa University
- Tibetan Buddhist institutions founded by the controversial Chögyam Trungpa Rinpoche (1939–1987), who arrived in the U.S. in 1970 and died of alcoholism

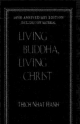

Order of Interbeing
- Vietnamese movement founded in the 1960s by Thich Nhat Hanh (1926–), a Thien (Zen) monk exiled for his political activities
- Based in Plum Village, a meditation community in southern France, Hanh travels the globe teaching "mindfulness retreats"
- Known to many for his book *Living Buddha, Living Christ*

FAMILY TREE OF FAR EASTERN RELIGIONS

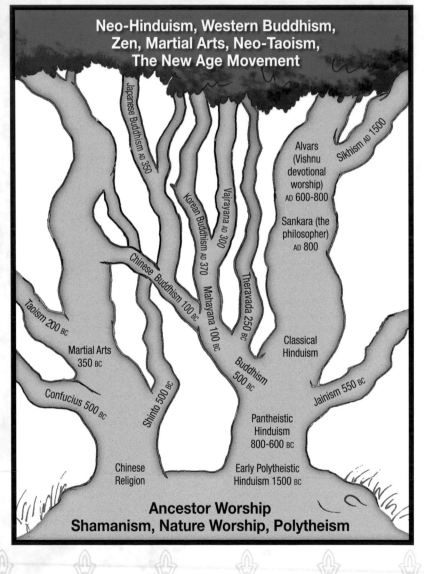

Neo-Hinduism, Western Buddhism,
Zen, Martial Arts, Neo-Taoism,
The New Age Movement

Japanese Buddhism AD 350

Sikhism AD 1500

Alvars
(Vishnu
devotional
worship)
AD 600-800

Sankara (the
philosopher)
AD 800

Korean Buddhism AD 370

Vajrayana AD 300

Chinese Buddhism 100 BC

Mahayana 100 BC

Theravada 250 BC

Taoism 200 BC

Martial Arts
350 BC

Classical
Hinduism

Confucius 500 BC

Shinto 500 BC

Buddhism
500 BC

Jainism 550 BC

Pantheistic
Hinduism
800-600 BC

Chinese
Religion

Early Polytheistic
Hinduism 1500 BC

Ancestor Worship
Shamanism, Nature Worship, Polytheism

TERMS AND DEFINITIONS

Ashram (Sanskrit, "abode," "residence")—term often used for the retreat center of a guru.

Bodhisattva (Sanskrit, "enlightened existence," "awakened being")—one who aspires to buddhahood but postpones his enlightenment to alleviate the suffering of others by his own merits.

Brahman (Sanskrit, "big," "expanded")—in theistic Hindu traditions, Brahman is God; in non-theistic traditions, Brahman is synonymous with the Universe (rather than an infinite, personal Creator).

Caste—a strict division of Indian society, based on differences of birth, which frequently determines one's status, profession, and occupation. Strongly related to the Vedic doctrine of karma.

Dharma (Sanskrit, "that which upholds and supports")—refers to the order which makes the complexity of the natural and spiritual worlds possible. Dharma is a central concept in Indian civilization, both Hindu and Buddhist, where it governs ideas about the proper conduct of living. It is symbolized by a wheel, seen in the center of the national flag of India.

Guru (Sanskrit, "teacher")—the highest rank of spiritual teacher in Hinduism, Jainism and Sikhism; one who has attained enlightenment or salvation after thousands of reincarnations.

Hindutva—Radical, nationalist movement advocating a Hindu theocracy in India.

Karma (Sanskrit, "act")—the spiritual principle of cause and effect, in which some kind of reward or punishment follows one's every act, whether good or bad. Thus, in Hinduism a person's past actions govern his present life, and future lives (reincarnations) are determined by past and present actions.

Lama—the Tibetan Buddhist equivalent of the Hindu word "guru"; commonly translated to mean "spiritual teacher."

Mantra (Sanskrit, "thought form")—a word or phrase, used repetitively in meditation to release the soul from bad karma and reincarnation.

Moksha (Sanskrit, "liberation")—release or salvation in Hinduism.

Monism—the teaching that all reality is one. Advaita (non-dual) Vedanta is a major school of Hindu philosophy that teaches this, emphasizing that what we commonly call reality is contingent, an illusion that hides the true reality beyond our contingent world.

New Age Movement—general term for the thousands of spiritual groups that have embraced and blended various elements of Asian religious philosophy and practice with popular psychology.

Nirvana (Sanskrit, "extinction")—Buddhist equivalent of moksha, or final liberation; literally means "blowing out," like a candle flame. The end of all personal existence.

Pantheism (Greek *pan*, "all," and *theos*, "God")—the teaching that God is not separate from his creation, but a vague impersonal force (similar to the atheistic scientific view that impersonal laws are the only foundation of reality).

Polytheism—The belief in many gods, such as the Greek or Roman pantheons. This is the most common form of ancient religion found worldwide, and still exists today in many forms.

Qi/Chi (Chinese, "air," "breath")—in Taoism, believed to be a universal life energy permeating the universe and one's body that can be manipulated for healing and spiritual benefits.

Reincarnation—the belief that each soul is reborn literally thousands of times before achieving liberation, or salvation. (Also called transmigration or metempsychosis)

Samsara (Sanskrit, "flow together")—the wandering that is the fate of the soul over many reincarnations.

Shamanism—the most primitive form of religion in the world, embracing a range of traditional beliefs and practices involving communication with the spirit world. Shares many similarities with crude forms of pantheism.

Tao (Chinese, "the way")—the way that life flows on both spiritual and material planes.

RESOURCES

The inclusion of a work does not necessarily mean endorsement of all its contents or of other works by the same author(s). A ♦ denotes a specifically Christian resource.

BOOKS
General
• *Asia's Religions: Christianity's Momentous Encounters with Paganism* by Lit-Sen Chang (P&R, 2000)♦

• *Buddhism, Taoism, and Other Far Eastern Religions* by J. Isumu Yamamoto (Zondervan, 1998)♦

• *The Compact Guide to World Religions* by Dean C. Halverson (Bethany, 1996)♦

• *Charts of World Religions* by H. Wayne House (Zondervan, 2006)♦

• *Dictionary of Contemporary Religion in the Western World,* edited by Christopher Partridge and Douglas Groothuis (InterVarsity, 2002)♦

• *Apologetics in the New Age: A Christian Critique of Pantheism* by David Clark and Norman Geisler (Baker, 1990)♦

• *Reincarnation vs. Resurrection* by John Snyder (Moody, 1984)

• *When the New Age Gets Old: Looking for a Greater Spirituality* by Vishal Mangalwadi (InterVarsity, 1992)♦

• *Eastern Definitions* by Edward Rice (Anchor, 1980)

Hinduism
• *Hinduism: A Brief Look at the Theology, History, Scriptures, and Social System with Comments on the Gospel in India* by H.L. Richard (William Carey, 2007)♦

• *Fulfillment of the Vedic Pilgrimage in the Lord Jesus Christ* by Acharya Daya Prakash Titus (OM Books, 2004)♦

• *Hinduism, TM and Hare Krishna* by J. Isamu Yamamoto (Zondervan, 1998)♦

• *The World of Gurus* by Vishal Mangalwadi (Cornerstone Press, 1992)♦

• *The Experience of Ultimate Truth* by Michael Graham (OM Books, 2001)♦

• *The Ochre Robe. An Autobiography* by Agehananda Bharati (Ross Erikson, 1980)

Buddhism
• *Beyond Buddhism* by J. Isamu Yamamoto (InterVarsity, 1982) ♦

• *The Lotus and the Cross: Jesus Talks with Buddha* by Ravi Zacharias (Multnomah, 2001)♦

• *What the Buddha Taught* by Walpola Rahula (Grove, 1994)

VIDEO/DVD
• *Phantom India*, directed by Louis Malle (Criterion, 2007)

• *Fear Is the Master* (Jeremiah Films, 1987)♦

• *Essentials of Faith: Hinduism* (Electric Sales/ Films Media Group, 2007)

• *Essentials of Faith: Buddhism* (Electric Sales/ Films Media Group, 2007)

• *A Separate Peace: Hinduism, Buddhism, Taoism, and Shintoism* (Films for the Humanities & Sciences, 1998)

• *Confucianism* (Public Affairs Television, 1996)

• *Jainism: Ascetics and Warriors* (Films Media Group, 1995)

• *World Sikhism Today* (Films Media Group, 1994)

POWERPOINT®
• *Christianity, Cults, and Religions* (Rose Publishing, Inc., 2010)♦

INTERNET
Karma to Grace♦
• www.karma2grace.org
Sonrise Center for Buddhist Studies♦
• www.sonrisecenter.org
World Religions: Comparative Analysis♦
• www.comparativereligion.com
Reincarnation: A Christian Critique of a New Age Doctrine♦
• www.ccel.us/reincarnation.toc.html

Principal Author: Mark Albrecht, M.A. Theology and World Religions
Editorial Consultants: H.L. Richard; J. Isamu Yamamoto; Brooks Alexander; András Szalai, Apológia Foundation; James Stephens, Sonrise Center for Buddhist Studies

Islam
& Christianity

Reaching Out to Muslims
Answering Misunderstandings

RELIGIOUS HISTORY

What Muslims Believe

Islam, the Original Religion
Muslims believe that Islam (meaning "submission" to Allah) is the original religion since the creation of Adam, the first prophet. Since the beginning of time, all people who submit to Allah are called Muslims. Over the centuries, Allah appointed thousands of prophets to warn and guide mankind. Prominent among them were *Ibrahim* (Abraham), *Musa* (Moses), *Dawud* (David), and *Isa Al Masih* (Jesus the Messiah).

Muhammad, the Final Prophet
Mankind habitually strayed from the way of Allah revealed through the prophets. About AD 610 in Arabia, Allah sent the last prophet, Muhammad, who united the Arab tribes and turned them from idolatry to Islam.

The Spread of Islam
After the death of Muhammad in AD 632, Sunni Islam rapidly spread from Arabia under the leadership of the first four "rightly guided" rulers (*caliphs*) who were close companions of Muhammad. Shia Islam began to rapidly spread through the teachings of "infallible" Imams from the bloodline of Muhammad. To Muslims, the military and economic expansion of Islam liberated people suffering under the corrupt Byzantine and Persian Empires.

What Christians Believe

Adam and Jesus
Christians also trace their religious history back to Adam, who brought the curse of sin upon all mankind (Gen. 1–3). In the Bible, Jesus is known as the second Adam, who came to remove this curse of sin (Rom. 5).

Abraham and Jesus
God's plan unfolded carefully over history. Abraham (*Ibrahim* in Arabic) was promised the blessing to carry out God's eternal purposes. He was blessed so he could be a blessing to all the families of the earth (Gen. 12:1–3; Gal. 3).

Jesus is the promised seed of Eve who would crush the head of Satan (*Shaytan* in Arabic; Gen. 3:15) and bring the blessing of the "Good News" (*Injil* in Arabic).

The Victory of Jesus
A great war has been raging throughout the Creation, a struggle in which Satan has twisted all good things—even religion—into weapons to discredit God. The decisive battle of this war was won on the cross when Jesus destroyed Satan's power and overcame the curse of sin. By rising from the dead, Jesus conquered death, a consequence of the curse, and thereby offers the blessing of eternal life to mankind.

How to Correct Misunderstandings

The Misunderstandings
Religious history between Christians and Muslims is covered with blood and war, much like all of human history. God's name has been used by both sides to justify murder and mayhem. Several key events in history continue to affect the perceptions of Christians and Muslims. These events include the Islamic expansion (7th–8th centuries), the Crusades (11th–13th centuries), the establishment of the state of Israel in 1948, the attack on the World Trade Center, the Gulf Wars of 1991 and 2003, and many other events.

Correcting the Misunderstandings
Historians have pointed out that these "holy wars" of history were more about economics than faith. Yet economic struggle cannot explain the intense hatred, cruelty and malicious evil of a Crusader, Nazi, or suicide bomber. Behind these horrors is a deeper spiritual war and a vindictive enemy, namely Satan. Christians and Muslims should not lose sight of Satan, the "enemy of souls." By recognizing the common enemy, Christians can create a context in which they can build relationships with Muslims.

WHO IS GOD?

What Muslims Believe

Allah Is One
The absolute oneness of Allah is primary to Muslims. The greatest sin is to associate any partner with him. This sin is called *shirk*. Muhammad's message advocating one God was courageous because idolatry was the established religion of Arabia. Muhammad challenged this system and finally prevailed with the message of monotheism. Islam is rooted in this commitment to the belief in one God.

Allah Cannot Be Compared
Allah is transcendent and cannot be compared to humans or any other created thing. Allah's character and attributes are revealed through his 99 Arabic names, the two most common being "The Merciful" and "The Compassionate." Allah is never described in Islam by using human family terms such as "father" or "son." In the Quran he reveals his will for mankind to obey, not his person for mankind to relate with and know.

Allah's Ultimate Attribute: His Will
Allah creates and sustains all life, spiritual and material. His will is absolute and cannot be questioned by his creation. He is our final judge without a mediator. The best chance on Judgment Day is for those who live lives of righteousness and submission to Allah's will— *Insha Allah* (God willing).

What Christians Believe

God: A Unity, Not a Unit
The Bible teaches that God is one, but he is a complex unity, not just a simple unit. He is completely unique, a personal God who existed in relationship from eternity.

God the Father, God the Son, God the Holy Spirit
Scripture reveals God as the ultimate Father, in name, character, and person, but always as the Creator, never with sexual references. God also reveals himself as the Eternal Word, who became flesh when the Holy Spirit overshadowed the Virgin Mary and conceived Jesus, the Messiah, who is also called the Son of God in the Bible. In his teaching, Jesus further reveals God the Holy Spirit, who was sent by the Father and himself. The Bible presents a mystery of three persons revealed as one God. Although the word "Trinity" is not in the Bible, the term captures Bible truths about God. The Father, the Son, and the Holy Spirit are God, not just three parts of God or three names for the same person. God reveals himself as a tri-unity.

God's Ultimate Attribute: His Love
The Bible says, "God is Love." This love existed from eternity as the Father loved the Son even before the foundation of the world. God's love is expressed through creation. God does not simply choose to love; his love chooses to act. "God so loved the world that he gave his one and only Son" (John 3:16).

How to Correct Misunderstandings

The Misunderstandings
Most Muslims consider Christians to be polytheists (people who believe in many gods) because of the Trinity. A popular misunderstanding of the Trinity is that Christians believe that a Father God had sex with a Mother God (Mary) to produce their "Son of God." No Christian believes this. Educated Muslims understand this false Trinity is not what Christians believe, but they still do not understand how the math can show God's unity. To them it is simple: 1+1+1=3; Father + Son + Holy Spirit = Three Gods. This is not what Christians believe.

Correcting the Misunderstandings
Rather than use an analogy of adding units (1+1+1=3), the Trinity has been explained as multiplied wholeness (1x1x1=1). The Bible says Jesus is the eternal "Word of God" revealed in flesh through the virgin birth. The Quran sets apart Jesus as "His (God's) Word" and "a Spirit from Him (God)" and mentions his virgin birth and miracles. Muslims also believe in the second coming of Jesus, because Jesus is called the "Sign of the Hour" in the Quran. Muslims like to point out how the Quran honors Jesus. Yet such positive references to Jesus in the Quran are few compared to the complete story of Jesus preserved by God in the New Testament.

HOLY SCRIPTURES

What Muslims Believe

The Only Trustworthy Scripture
According to Muslims, there is only one trustworthy Holy Scripture, the Quran ("a text to recite"). Many prophets before Muhammad were also given Allah's Word, among them: *Musa* (Moses) given the *Taurat* (Torah), *Dawud* (David) given the *Zabur* (Psalms), and *Isa* (Jesus) given the *Injil* (Gospel). However, Muslims are taught that all these writings were corrupted. Allah appointed Muhammad to receive the Quran in order to correct this corruption.

How Muslims Got the Quran
In AD 610, Allah sent the archangel Gabriel (*Jibrail* in Arabic) to Muhammad in Mecca, Saudi Arabia. Over the next 22 years, Allah "sent down" revelations to Gabriel who dictated them to Muhammad with the command to recite it to others. Shortly after Muhammad's death in AD 632, his followers gathered the texts of different lengths into 114 chapters (*Sura* in Arabic). The third caliph, Uthman, had scholars compile an official Quran, in written form, and had all other variant texts burned.

The Quran Today
The Quran is considered divine in its original Arabic form, and Muslims memorize and recite it only in this pure language.

What Christians Believe

How Christians Got the Bible
Followers of Jesus believe the Bible is the authoritative, inspired word of God, composed of 66 different books, transmitted through at least 40 prophets, apostles, and holy men. The first 39 books, written before the coming of Christ, are called the Old Testament. The Old Testament was written over many centuries by various authors in diverse cultures using the Hebrew and Aramaic languages. The remaining 27 books after Christ are called the New Testament. They were written in Greek, the dominant language of the 1st century. The New Testament contains collections of eyewitness reports of the life and teachings of Jesus, followed by a history of his disciples over the next 50 years, including letters from his apostles and a vision of the end times called the "Revelation."

Inspiration
The Christian view of inspiration is that God "breathed" his Word through many people (mostly inspiring, rarely dictating). Therefore the Bible reflects cultures as diverse as Abraham's nomadic lifestyle to the royal court of King David. The result is a book of beautiful human diversity interwoven with divine unity.

How to Correct Misunderstandings

The Misunderstandings
Muslims feel sorry that Christians follow a corrupted book and most Muslims avoid the Bible. Even among Western-educated Muslims, the great diversity of Bible versions and translations adds to their belief that the Bible is corrupted.

Correcting the Misunderstandings
Muhammad did not question the accuracy of the Bible; he criticized contemporary Jews and Christians for misinterpreting or not obeying their existing Scriptures. The accusation that the text of the Bible had been corrupted came centuries after Muhammad, at a time when Muslim scholars realized there were contradictions between the Quran and the Bible. Yet the Quran points to the Bible as truth to obey many times. The text of the Bible is better preserved than the writings of any ancient author. Furthermore, the discovery of the Dead Sea Scrolls confirmed the reliability of the Bible.

PROPHETS

What Muslims Believe

Muhammad, the Seal of the Prophets
To Muslims, the Prophet Muhammad, called the "seal of the prophets," is the last of over 124,000 prophets going back to Adam. His name means "praised one," and he is commended by Allah in the Quran.

Muhammad, the Reformer
Mecca was a center of idol worship in AD 610 when Muhammad first challenged the people to forsake idolatry and embrace Islam. Most Meccans rejected his message and many began to persecute the early Muslims, causing them to flee to the town of Medina in AD 622. (This flight is known as the *hijara* and marked the first year on the Islamic calendar.) Medina was more receptive to Muhammad, and from this city, through battles and diplomacy, Islam was spread to the entire Arabian Peninsula within only a few years after Muhammad's death in AD 632.

Muhammad, the Perfect Example to Follow
Muslims try to follow Muhammad's example known as his *sunna* ("trodden path" or "customs") in every detail possible. Everything is prescribed, from ritual washings before prayer to hygienic practices in the bathroom. Such detailed behavior is known through large collections of *hadith*, accounts of Muhammad's life, words, and behavior passed on by his early followers.

What Christians Believe

Old Testament Prophecy
New Testament writers proclaimed Jesus as the fulfillment of the Law of Moses (*Taurat*) and the predictions of Old Testament prophets. These prophets are quoted in the New Testament. For instance, Matthew quotes various prophets concerning Jesus' birth in Bethlehem (Mic. 5:2), his mother being a virgin (Isa. 7:14), and even the killing of baby boys by King Herod (Jer. 31:15). The prophets also detail the suffering, death, and resurrection of Jesus (Isa. 53; Ps. 16:8–11). The Bible points out that God carefully planned and carried out the details of the coming of Jesus in history (Luke 24:27; Acts 3:18).

Christ's Warning about False Teachers
The Bible contains numerous warnings about false teachers and prophets. Jesus predicts the end times will be full of these (Matt. 24: 11). Therefore, every teaching must be judged against the truth already revealed in the Bible. Jesus also promised that the Holy Spirit ("the Spirit of Truth") would guide truth seekers into all truth (John 14–16).

How to Correct Misunderstandings

The Misunderstandings
In conversation with Muslims, do not attack Muhammad. Since so much is determined by imitating their prophet, to insult Muhammad is to attack their entire life and culture.

Correcting the Misunderstandings
It is wise to find common ground and agree that Muhammad has much in common with Old Testament prophets. Like David and Solomon, he was a political and military leader with multiple wives. Like Moses and Joshua, he united tribes and led them in battle. Like Elijah and many other prophets, he destroyed idols and confronted the corrupt political and economic powers of his day.

Just as Old Testament prophets looked forward to the coming Messiah, Muhammad looked back with respect and admiration to Jesus as the Messiah. The Quran calls *Isa Al Masih* (Jesus) "His (God's) Word" and "a Spirit from Him (God)" (Surah 4:171). It affirms Jesus' virgin birth and special role in the end times, though not in the biblical sense.

Followers of Jesus do not have to insult or embrace Muhammad in order to exalt the Messiah. It is important to lift up Jesus, not tear down Muhammad.

PRACTICES AND RITUALS

What Muslims Believe

The Five Pillars
The ritual practices of Islam are the pillars of their religious system. Although beliefs are important, the substance of their religion is the accomplishment of these five pillars.
- Confessing the Faith (*Shahada*)
- Prayer (*Salat*)
- Fasting (*Sawm*)
- Giving of Alms (*Zakat*)
- Pilgrimage to Mecca (*Hajj*)

The Muslim's objective is to follow Muhammad's pattern (his exact words, motions, and timing) found in the sunna as they accomplish the pillars.

Jihad
Some Muslims also consider "struggle (*Jihad*) in Allah's way" central to their faith. This struggle could be internal (a struggle in the soul to do the right thing) or external (self-defense against attackers of Islam or Muslims). The interpretation of jihad can determine the difference between moderate and radical Muslims.

Judgment Day
Their belief in the nature of the final Judgment Day motivates Muslims to faithfully accomplish these pillars. In the Quran, these practices are of great importance.

What Christians Believe

The Gift of Salvation
The Bible teaches that salvation is a gift from God through faith in Jesus Christ (*Isa Al Masih*) and there are no rituals or practices that anyone can do in order to get right with God (Eph. 2:8–9).

Jesus' Seven Commands
Even though no one can be saved by good works, followers of Jesus serve him, imitate him, and do what he commanded because they are filled with the Holy Spirit. Jesus said, "If you love me, keep my commands" (John 14:15) and that this "burden is light" (Matt. 11:30).

He gave seven specific commands:
- Repent and Believe (a turn of heart)
- Love God and Others (greatest command)
- Pray (as a lifestyle, from the heart)
- Celebrate the Lord's Supper (remember Jesus)
- Be Baptized (with water)
- Give (with a joyful heart)
- Make Disciples (among all peoples)

Making disciples involves worship, fellowship, fasting, studying Scripture, and sharing the good news. Jesus said that his disciples would be recognized by their love for one another (John 13:35).

How to Correct Misunderstandings

The Misunderstandings
A Muslim can be confused by Christian symbols and rituals, such as the cross (considered a military symbol to Muslims) and the Lord's Supper when using wine (alcohol is prohibited in Islam). Christians are confused by some of the Muslim rituals as well.

Correcting the Misunderstandings
If Christians and Muslims can communicate and completely understand the meaning behind these symbols and rituals, meaningful relationships can be built and truth-sharing can take place.

Following the Sermon on the Mount (Matt. 5–7) is perhaps the best way for Christians to imitate Jesus and share with Muslims. The Sermon on the Mount challenges all followers of Jesus to live a righteous lifestyle of humility and love.

Muslims need grace-motivated Christian friends who follow the disciplines of Jesus. Jesus calls his followers to pray as a lifestyle, frequently and effectively. By confronting evil and bringing healing, believers can introduce Christ to their Muslim friends.

SALVATION AND PARADISE

What Muslims Believe

Reward and Penalty
The Quran says, "For those who reject Allah, there is a terrible penalty: but for those who believe and work righteous deeds, there is forgiveness and a magnificent reward" (Surah 35:7). This great reward is *janna*, a garden paradise, an eternal place of sensual and spiritual pleasures.

No Savior, but Mercy Is Possible
In Islam, there is no savior. That is not to say salvation is impossible, for Allah is merciful and compassionate. He can always forgive—for Allah's will is supreme—but he is primarily the judge. There are many descriptive warnings about hellfire and punishment in the Quran.

Judgment Day: A Motivation to Righteous Deeds
All people should fear Judgment Day, in which each person's deeds will be weighed on a scale. "Recording angels" keep a list of every deed, both good and bad. Islamic teachers assign credits to deeds related to the pillars of Islam. It is unthinkable for many Muslims to abandon their accumulation of credits and trust a Savior.

Guarantee of Paradise?
Islamist terrorists interpret the Quran to suggest that paradise is guaranteed for jihad martyrs. Most Muslim scholars and leaders reject the terrorists' definitions of jihad and martyrdom.

What Christians Believe

Judgment Day
Christians believe that after death, all people await the final Judgment when both believers and unbelievers will be resurrected. All will be judged according to the deeds they have done, but believers will be saved because God removed the record that contained the charges against them. He destroyed it by nailing it to the cross of Jesus (Col. 2:14). This would remove the list of bad deeds kept by any Muslim's "recording angel."

The Gift of Salvation
Even if one's list of good deeds outweighs their list of bad deeds, this would not make them acceptable to God. The Bible says this would only cause boasting and pride, as though someone could impress God by his or her good deeds (Eph. 2:8–10). Instead, God has credited us with the righteousness of Christ, so salvation is a gift, not earned by anyone, not even martyrs, but bought with a great price (Jesus' blood).

A Renewed Relationship with God
In addition to this great gift, God the Father adopts those he saves into his family so they may live with Jesus in heaven. To be saved involves being "born again" into a new relationship with God (John 3:5).

How to Correct Misunderstandings

The Misunderstandings
Thinking about Allah as Father is unacceptable for all Muslims (Surah 112:3). Any negative view of the earthly father role will twist one's view of God. In Western cultures, parenting trends err toward permissiveness (more love than discipline). In the East, fathers tend to be negligent or authoritarian (more discipline than love). God is a Father, who shows both love and discipline. He wants loving followers, not slaves or spoiled children.

Correcting the Misunderstandings
This view of fatherhood makes it easier to relate to God as Father and to come to him as a humble child, ready to be loved and disciplined. Jesus said one must enter God's kingdom as a little child.

The final book of the Bible describes the future scene of a huge family gathering with many from every tribe, tongue, people, and ethnic group gathered around the throne of God (Rev. 5). Boasting of good deeds would be unthinkable, because Jesus, the Lamb of God, sits upon the throne. Everyone in this great crowd honors Jesus as their substitute sacrifice, just as God pictured beforehand when he provided a ram to die in place of Abraham's son (Gen. 22).

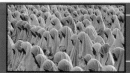

ROLE OF WOMEN

What Muslims Believe

The Perspective of Muslim Women
Muslim women generally consider themselves protected and satisfied within their culture. Their fulfilling social life is usually gender-separated and happens primarily within extended families and some close neighbors.

The Protection of Muslim Women
Women are valued in the Quran. Muhammad brought an end to the practice of female infanticide, widely practiced before his time, and he gave women the right to inherit. The honor of women is a major concern in Muslim societies. The reputation of the family is linked with the women. Islam helps maintain roles and expectations that predate Muhammad. The modest dress code is intended to protect women when outside the home. Muslim women do not need to wear a veil or loose clothes at home or when only women are present.

Polygamy
Since marriage and child bearing are highly valued in Islamic society, polygamy is allowed and yet controlled. Islam limits a man to four wives and requires equal treatment for each.

What Christians Believe

The Perspective of Christian Women
Christians believe that the Bible teaches that both man and woman were created in God's image, had a direct relationship with God, and shared jointly the responsibilities of bringing up children and ruling over the created order (Gen. 1:26–28). Christian husbands and wives are to mutually submit to one another. Women are to respect their husbands; husbands are to sacrificially and selflessly love their wives, just as Jesus Christ loves his church (Eph. 5:21–25).

The Protection of Christian Women
Christian women are to dress modestly (1 Tim. 2:9), and all followers of Jesus are to flee from sexual immorality (1 Cor. 6:18).

Not Conforming to the World
Followers of Jesus believe that they must be transformed by renewing their minds and avoid conforming to the patterns of the secular world (Rom. 12:2). Problems arise when Christians adapt to the Western secular culture more than to the Bible. When this happens there is a decline in morality which leads to an increase in sexual immorality, drunkenness, deceit, selfishness, rage, and other sins.

How to Correct Misunderstandings

The Misunderstandings
Western values conflict with Muslims regarding women perhaps more than any other category. There are several problems in Muslim societies in regard to women. However, secularism and women's liberation have brought the "Christian" West several problems as well.

Correcting the Misunderstandings
Christians, often focused on the plight of Muslim women, fail to see that many Western "solutions" are more to be feared than the problems they address. Many Muslim women prefer their lifestyle to lonely singleness, sexual exploitation, and the desire for money that makes home and family unimportant.

Societies long dominated by Islam have problems which need to be addressed, but before Christians can address these issues they must deal with their own cultural problems. As Jesus said, "You hypocrite, first take the plank out of your own eye, and then you will see clearly to remove the speck from your brother's eye" (Matt. 7:5).

RELIGION AND CULTURE

What Muslims Believe

The Muslim Holistic Worldview
Muslims understand religion as a whole and integrated way of life. Secular, Christian-influenced cultures can confuse and even anger Muslims who see things through their holistic worldview. They often view "Hollywood sexuality" as "Christian," or a military action as a "Crusade." To them, the cross is a military symbol.

The Islamic Community
In Islam, brotherhood and consensus is emphasized, and individualism is avoided. The "community of the faithful" is responsible to enforce the moral code. This can explain how a lone Muslim, outside a community support structure, does not feel as guilty when breaking the code. However, bringing shame on his family or community would be a great sin.

Avoiding shame and protecting honor are primary motivations of most Muslims. Shame and honor are community-related, as contrasted to an individual sense of guilt.

Radical Muslims, known as Islamists or Jihadists, use this sense of community honor and shame to recruit and motivate their followers.

What Christians Believe

The Western Worldview
Followers of Jesus believe that they are to impact culture for Christ by going into all parts of the world to bring the message of Jesus to the people that live there (Matt. 28:19–20). In the West, a division exists between culture and religion. Religion is separated from government, and some people object to any influence of religion on state institutions and symbols.

Community in the West
Followers of Jesus do influence Western culture and institutions, but they seem to be a shrinking influence. Western culture affirms individualism and some people avoid community responsibility. Tolerance of sin and unbiblical practices continue to dilute the true Christian message; evolutionism and atheism also continue to influence the increasingly secular West. Only a minority of those in the West consider themselves followers of Jesus Christ. Most simply consider themselves Christian by name only, and do not follow the teaching of the Bible, of which they are largely ignorant. Generally, Western culture does not have a sense of the "community of the faithful."

How to Correct Misunderstandings

The Misunderstandings
Time magazine ran a cover article asking the question, "Should Christians Convert Muslims?" The artwork featured a militant-looking clenched fist holding a metal cross, reminiscent of a Crusader's sword. This imagery correctly symbolizes some typical Muslim misunderstandings, especially when viewed with the cigarette advertisement on the back cover. The advertisement features a sensual goddess-like model with men fawning at her feet. These pictures display some fears of Muslims: to be dominated militarily and corrupted morally by "Christianity."

Correcting the Misunderstandings
The challenge is to present a correct view of the cross. The movie, "The Passion of the Christ," has been seen by Muslims all over the world. They have seen the cross as a symbol of suffering, not as a military or political icon. Followers of Jesus, through their words and actions, are called to show Muslims that God loves all people so much that Jesus died on the cross for their sins. (Islam denies Jesus' death; claims that he was lifted up to heaven and a substitute died instead of him.) Jesus also defeated Satan and death by rising from the grave. He made it possible for all of God's children to live with him forever. This "good news" should be attractive to Muslims.

The Do's and Don'ts of Reaching Out to Muslims

Do make it clear you are a follower of Christ, by your loving words and righteous lifestyle.

Don't assume your Muslim friend understands your meaning of "Christian."

Do take time to build a relationship. Practice hospitality.

Don't be surprised if you are rejected at first. It is best to offer Muslim friends store-bought sweets and to avoid anything with pork or alcohol.

Do approach your encounters as a learner. Ask questions.

Don't take notes and treat Muslim friends like an academic project.

Do correct their misunderstandings of your beliefs.

Don't argue. If they want to debate with a Christian, refer them to the website www.debate.org.uk/.

Do talk about Jesus. Use his title, *Isa Al Masih*.

Don't insult the prophet Muhammad.

Do pray out loud with your Muslim friends. Ask if you can pray for their practical needs, healing, and worries. Look for opportunities and pray in Jesus' name.

Don't start your prayer with "Our Father…" because Muslims have a misunderstanding about the fatherhood of God (as sexual). Wait until you correct this misunderstanding before using "Father" or "Abba." At first address your prayer to "Almighty God" or "Lord God."

Do use your right hand in giving and receiving gifts.

Don't use your left hand for eating food (especially when learning to eat with your hands). The left hand is used for toilet cleaning; the right hand for eating.

Do treat your Bible with respect. Store it high on a shelf. Some wrap it in a beautiful cloth.

Don't put your Bible on the floor or in the bathroom as reading material. Many Muslims are superstitious about the bathroom.

Do be gender-sensitive: interact man to man, woman to woman.

Don't allow any compromising situation, even just to protect from a possible rumor. An Arab proverb says, "A man and woman alone together are three with the devil."

Do observe body language. Take your shoes off when entering a home or place of prayer (especially if you see shoes at the threshold).

Don't sit so that the sole of your foot or shoe is facing someone. Women, don't look men directly in the eye, or at least quickly avert your glance.

Do practice modesty, even among Westernized Muslims. For women this is very important since family honor is tied to their behavior and reputation.

Don't assume Muslims think the same as you, even if they dress the same.

Helpful Words and Definitions

Although 80% of Muslims do not converse in Arabic, all Muslims use some Arabic terms and phrases because Islam requires uniformity. For example, the Arabic names of all their prophets, including Jesus Christ, are easily recognized by Muslims. The same is true with the universal Muslim greeting, "Salaam alaykum," because Muhammad required it to be used. For a Christian to use some Muslim-friendly words can help avoid misunderstandings, but it can also lead to the impression that one is interested in converting to Islam. This is a risk worth taking in order to communicate the Good News as a truly positive message, not as a corrupting influence. The following phrases and terms are among the most helpful in using with Muslims. It is good to ask your Muslim friend to help you pronounce these Arabic terms.

Bismillah (Bis-mi-LAH)—"In the name of Allah." An invocation frequently used by Muslims. The longer version, Bismillah ar-Rahman ar-Rahim, means "in the name of Allah, the Compassionate, the Merciful." As a way to honor their Muslim friends, Christians can ask for help to memorize and appropriately speak this Arabic phrase because similar terms are deeply rooted in biblical understanding.

Hadith (Hah-DEETH)—Thousands of reports of sayings or behaviors of Muhammad which set a precedent for Muslim practice and becomes the basis of Sharia law.

Ibrahim (E-brah-HEEM)—"Abraham"

Injil (In-JEEL)—Refers to the "book given to Jesus" and comes from the Greek word *evangelion*, meaning "good news." Muslims do not believe that there is an Injil remaining on the earth that has not been corrupted. Christians often refer to the Gospels or a single Gospel as "the Injil" when conversing with Muslims.

Insha Allah (In-SHA-al-lah)—"God willing." This common phrase is often tagged onto a sentence expressing hope or intention, and sometimes resignation to destiny. It is an expression of Allah's ultimate attribute: his absolute will.

Isa Al Masih (EE-saw-all-Mah-SEE)—"Jesus the Mes-si-ah." The word "Ma-sih" is similar to the Hebrew word. "Isa" for "Jesus" is an obscure version of the Arab Christians' *Yasu* (from Hebrew *Yeshua*).

Salaam Alaykum (Sa-LAAM Ah-LAY-kum)—"Peace be upon you." It is virtually identical to the Aramaic phrase Jesus spoke when appearing to the disciples after his resurrection (Luke 24:36; John 20:19).

Sharia (Sha-REE-ah)—"Path to water." Islamic religious and civil law which is based upon the Sunna, Quran, and Hadith. Sharia is a guide to everyday life and salvation. Sunni scholars developed four schools of interpretation named after their founders: Hanafi (d. 767), Maliki (d. 795), Shafii (d. 820), and Hanbali (d. 855). Shia have their own similar schools.

Shaytan (Satan) (Shay-TAAN)—An evil *Jinn* (fire-born spirits in Arabic folklore), not a rebellious angel. The Quran uses this term to refer to mischievous behavior (like devilish).

Shiite or Shia (SHE-ite or SHE-ah)—"The party of Ali" (10% worldwide) that believes that the proper successor to Muhammad should be his blood relative, beginning with Ali. The Sunni-Shia split happened shortly after Muhammad's death in a violent dispute about who should lead the Muslim community.

Shirk (SHIRK)—"Associating." Idolatry or blasphemy. Making others equal to God, an unpardonable sin, like disbelief (*qufr*).

Sufi (SOO-fee)—Muslim mystics, who can be either Sunni or Shia, range from storytellers seeking to love Allah and his wisdom to those inducing trances through chanting the names of Allah or dancing (as seen in "whirling dervishes").

Sunna (SOO-nah)—"Trodden path" of Muhammad and his close companions. The Sunna (Muhammad's examples) becomes the basis of Sharia law.

Sunni (SOO-nee)—"One on the path;" how the majority of Muslims (90% worldwide) identify themselves as contrasted to Shiite.

Taurat of Musa (Tor-AT MOO-sah)—"Torah of Moses," the book given to Moses. The first five books of the Bible.

Tawheed (Toe-HEED) "Oneness." A term used to refer to the absolute oneness of Allah.

Zabur of Dawud (Zah-BOOR DAU-ood)—"Psalms of David," the book given to David, the Psalms.

Notes and References

Allah The proper pre-Islamic Arabic name for God, used even today by Arabic-speaking Christians as well as by Muslims. Scholars think the word "Allah" is originally a compound of *al-ilah* ("the god"). Although all Muslims use the Arabic name "Allah," only 20% are native Arabic speakers. Muslims with other native languages have still another name for God. For example, Farsi-speaking peoples use "Khodah" to mean God. Bible translators usually employ the native language term for God, the uncreated Creator.

Muslim An Arabic term derived from the same root as the word for peace (*salam*). Note that the trilateral root _S_L_M_ is shared by all these related terms: SALAM, ISLAM, MUSLIM. The root and its derivatives are very similar to the Hebrew word "Shalom," which means peace.

Baraka Literally means "blessing," a term that communicates well to Muslims. Baraka is a central biblical theme first introduced by God to Abraham (*Ibrahim*) in Genesis 12:1–3, and extended to all believers of all nations (Gal. 3:6–9).

Pillars The five pillars of religion (*arkan-ad-din* in Arabic) are referred to by their Arabic names by all Muslims, regardless of their native language.

- **Confessing the Faith** (*Shahada*) is a public statement said in Arabic which means, "There is no God but Allah and Muhammad is His Messenger." Making this confession is the first step in becoming a Muslim. Islam requires that everyone say this confession in Arabic.

- **Prayer** (*Salat*) is a set ritual to be done five specific times every day (sometimes combined in three sessions), memorized in Arabic, with ritual washings before each sequence. The head must be covered, the body pointed in the direction of Mecca, and the motions and prostrations must be followed for the prayers to be valid.

- **Fasting** (*Sawm*) is an annual community event for all Muslims (except children, pregnant women, and travelers). The fast lasts the entire lunar month known as Ramadan, and involves abstinence from all food, water, and sex during daylight hours. At sunset, when the daily fast ends, there is a special meal (*iftar*) and another just before sunrise. In Muslim dominated countries there is often a shift to a more nocturnal schedule with more sleep during the daytime and feasting at night.

- **Giving of Alms** (*Zakat*) is obligatory giving of 2.5% of a Muslim's wealth, primarily to the poor and for the support of religious and educational institutions or the self-defense of the Islamic community.

- **Pilgrimage to Mecca** (*Hajj*) is to be carried out at least once in a lifetime, providing a Muslim can afford it. Uniformity is enforced in the manner of dressing—in a white garment—to shaving the head (for the men). The objective is to strengthen Arabic-Abrahamic identity by recalling the story of Hagar and Ishmael and the union of all Muslims by circulating around the ancient Arabic-Abrahamic religious center (*Kaaba*). Great claims are made for gaining multiplied credits as well as removing the weight of sins in preparation of the scale of Judgment Day.

Featured Photos and Artwork

Ring (page 59): Afghanistan is famous for its dark blue lapis lazuli gemstone, set here in a hand-crafted silver ring featuring a clear symbol of the Trinity. Although its meaning may be lost in this Muslim nation, this is an ancient Christian symbol of Tri-unity and eternity.

Arabic translations of the Injil (Gospel of Luke) and Taurat (Genesis) (page 60): Muslims treat holy books with great respect, putting them on special reading stands and some wrap them in protective cloths.

Muhammad and the Archangel Gabriel (page 61): Copy of a sixteenth-century Turkish manuscript called *The Progress of the Prophet*. Notice the prophet is veiled to avoid sacrilege.

The Kaaba (page 62): The Kaaba is a cube-shaped building in Mecca toward which Muslims pray. Muslims believe the Kaaba was an altar used by *Ibrahim* (Abraham)

Time magazine cover and advertisement (page 65): This magazine cover and advertisement on the back display a common misunderstanding about Western culture.

Primary author: Rev. Bruce Green (MA, Biola University, 1983) has been building bridges since 1983 between Muslims and a consortium of evangelical churches. **Contributor:** Andras Szalai, PhD

Special thanks to: Amal Bejjani, Anne Dinnan (Coordinator of Resource Development Muslim Ministries), and Labib Madanat (Executive Secretary, Palestinian Bible Society). **Photos/art:** Peter Commandeur

10 Questions & Answers on
Jehovah's
Witnesses

Is the New World Translation Reliable?

Are Only 144,000 People Going to Heaven?

Is the Trinity a Pagan Doctrine?

Is Jesus Christ Really God?

1 Q. How Did Jehovah's Witnesses Begin?

The Watchtower Claims...

Apostasy and Restoration

Jehovah's Witnesses claim that Christianity fell into general apostasy under Emperor Constantine in the 4th century AD. To restore pure worship in the last days, God appointed Charles Taze Russell (1852–1916), who established the Watchtower organization to provide spiritual truth for Jehovah's true worshipers through literature such as *The Watchtower* and *Awake!* magazines.

Adventist Influence

In the 1870s Russell rejected the concept of eternal torment and joined a group of "Second Adventists" who taught that the wicked do not suffer in hell, but cease to exist when they die. In 1879 Russell split from the Adventists and began publishing *Zion's Watch Tower and Herald of Christ's Presence*, incorporating many Adventist beliefs such as rejection the Trinity, eternal punishment, and the immortality of the soul. Russell also declared that Christ's "invisible presence" (not physical return) began in 1874 and would end human government and restore paradise to earth by 1914.

The Bible Teaches...

No General Apostasy

The Bible warns that in the last days some will depart from the faith (1 Tim. 4:1), but nowhere does it indicate that true Christianity would almost entirely fall away. Instead, Jesus promised that the "gates of hell" would never "overpower" his church (Matt. 16:18). The apostle Paul also proclaimed that God would receive glory in his church "throughout all generations" (Eph. 3:21).

Russell and the Bible

Scripture warns of a time when people "will not endure sound doctrine; but wanting to have their ears tickled, they will accumulate for themselves teachers in accordance to their own desires" (2 Tim. 4:3). Russell did this when he rejected the clear teaching of Scripture on eternal punishment (Matt. 10:28; 25:46; Luke 16:22–29; Rev. 20:10–15).

You Should Also Know...

Charles Taze Russell, founder

Troublesome Teachings

- Russell shifted the date for the end of the world from 1914 to 1915, then to 1918.
- Early Watchtower publications claimed that the Great Pyramid in Giza, Egypt, foretold dates for the end of the world, based on the lengths of its passageways. When these dates failed, the measurements were lengthened to accommodate new dates.
- Russell's successor was "Judge" Joseph Rutherford (1869–1942). He moved the date for the world's end to 1925, proclaimed that "Millions Now Living Will Never Die!" and built a house in San Diego for the anticipated return of Abraham, Isaac, Jacob, and other "ancient worthies."
- Rutherford taught that Jehovah "governs his universe" from Alcyone (a star system in the Pleiades cluster) and that black skin is a sign of the biblical curse on Cain.

2. Is God's True Name Really "Jehovah"?

The Watchtower Claims...

God's Personal Name

Calling God by his personal name— "Jehovah"—is of utmost importance. In the Watchtower's *New World Translation*, Psalm 83:18 reads: "That people may know that You, whose name is Jehovah, You alone are the Most High over all the earth." God's true followers can be identified by their use of "Jehovah" in their prayers, congregational singing, preaching, and Bible study. (Many Witnesses believe that if "Jehovah" is not invoked in prayer, the prayer may go to some other "god.")

God's Name in Scripture

Where nearly all other Bibles have "Lord" for God's name in the Old Testament, the *New World Translation* (NWT) renders it "Jehovah"— and even "restores" the divine name to the New Testament. This is evidence of the Watchtower's superiority to apostate Christendom. Proverbs 30:6 and Revelation 22:18–19 warn about those who would "add" or "take away" from God's Word; thus, Bibles that take away God's name by inserting "Lord" where it should say "Jehovah" are not trustworthy.

The Tetragrammaton, God's holy name as written in Hebrew

You Should Also Know...

Pronouncing the Name

The original, ancient manuscripts of the Old Testament were written in Hebrew—all in consonants, with no vowels. Later, when scholars added vowel points (markings to indicate pronunciation) to the Hebrew text, no one could be sure what vowels to put into God's name, which is transliterated in English as "YHWH." For centuries, when Scripture was read aloud by the Jews their custom has been to keep God's name

The Bible Teaches...

"Father" or "Jehovah"?

Though the Jehovah's Witnesses insist on calling God "Jehovah" in prayer, in the Lord's Prayer Jesus tells us to address God as "Father" (Matt. 6:9–13). (The name "Jehovah" does not appear in the Lord's Prayer, even in the NWT.) For Jesus, sanctifying God's name has more to do with honoring what it stands for than with pronouncing his name. He also shows that his disciples are now "adopted" into God's family. As "sons" of God they now have the right to call God "Father," whereas before they could only refer to him by his formal titles or name.

"Jehovah" in the New Testament

The Watchtower may be justified in rendering God's name as "Jehovah" in its version of the Old Testament, but not in inserting it 237 times in the New Testament. Of the 5,000 Greek manuscripts we possess today of the New Testament, not a single one contains God's full name. (The expression "Hallelujah" in Revelation 19:1-6 contains a shortened form of the name, "Jah.") In this respect, the NWT is guilty of adding to God's Word by inserting his name where it doesn't belong in the text. By inserting "Jehovah" where there is no evidence that the New Testament writers used God's name, the *New World Translation* distorts Jesus' identity by creating an artificial distinction between him and Jehovah God.

holy by saying "Adonai" (Lord) instead of pronouncing it. So, scholars chose to insert the vowel points of "Adonai" (Lord) into "YHWH," rendering it "YaHoWaH" or "Jehovah."

Is the Trinity Really a Pagan Doctrine?

The Watchtower Claims...

Worshiping Three Gods

Christendom's idea of three persons in one God is really a pagan doctrine, comparable to the triadic "gods" of Babylonian and Egyptian mythology. There is no biblical or ancient church basis for the Trinity doctrine, and no such term appears in the Bible. Instead, the Father (Jehovah) and his Son (Jesus) are two separate "gods"— Jesus is an inferior "god" serving under Jehovah (who is the "only true God"). The holy spirit is God's "invisible active force," comparable to radio waves or electricity.

You Should Also Know...

Misconception of the Trinity

The "Trinity" is the historic Christian view that the Father, Son, and Holy Spirit are three distinct persons revealed in one God. Many people, including the Witnesses, mistakenly believe that in the Trinity, Jesus and the Father are somehow the same person. Pointing to biblical passages that speak of Christ's distinction from the Father and his submission to the will of the Father, they proclaim that the Trinity doctrine contradicts Scripture.

The Trinity in History

The Watchtower Society claims that ancient Christian leaders rejected the Trinity; however, this is not true. For example, in its pamphlet *Should You Believe in the Trinity?* the Watchtower claims that Clement of Alexandria considered Jesus "not equal" to the Father. Yet Clement actually praised Jesus as "the Divine Word, He that is truly most manifest Deity, He that is made equal to the Lord of the universe." He further explained: "I understand nothing else than the Holy Trinity to be meant; for the third is the Holy Spirit, and the Son is the

The Bible Teaches...

The Trinity in Scripture

Evidence of God's tri-unity is seen throughout Scripture. The Father (1 Pet. 1:2), Son (John 1:1; 20:28), and Holy Spirit (Acts 5:3–4) are each called "God." Yet, they operate distinctly from one another, indicating personhood. Given the emphatic declaration that there is only one true God (for example, Deut. 6:4; John 17:3), we conclude that this "one God" exists in three unique Persons. Many passages ascribe divine attributes to all three Persons or list the three together (as in the words used for baptism in Matthew 28:19).

Answering Objections

Most objections focus on the "subjection" of the Son to the will of the Father and Jesus' statement that the Father is "greater" than he (John 14:28). Philippians 2:5–11 explains how Christ subjected himself in taking on human nature to redeem mankind. While Jesus was on earth, the Father was in a "greater" position than he, but position doesn't denote an inferior nature.

second, by whom all things were made according to the will of the Father.... the Word itself, that is, the Son of God, who being, by equality of substance, one with the Father, is eternal and uncreated" (*The Ante-Nicene Fathers,* vol. 2, pp. 202, 468, 574).

The triquetra, an ancient symbol representing the Trinity

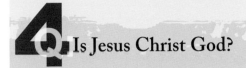

Q: Is Jesus Christ God?

The Watchtower Claims...

Jesus = Michael the Archangel

Jesus began his existence as Michael the Archangel (whose name means "Who is like God?"). He was the first one created and used by Jehovah God to create everything else. Since Satan (a created angel) is called "god" at 2 Corinthians 4:4, we may also regard Jehovah's spirit Son, Jesus, as a "god."

Earth and Beyond

When Jesus came to earth, he ceased to exist as Michael and became merely a perfect human. At death, Jesus' human body was "disposed" of by God's power, and Michael rose from the dead as the "resurrected Jesus Christ." Since angels are invisible, Jesus fabricated physical bodies resembling his original body to convince his disciples that he had risen from the dead. Since 1914, when Jesus' "invisible presence" on earth began, he has been reigning from heaven, awaiting the future battle of Armageddon in which he will rid the earth of human governments and set up "Paradise" under "Jehovah's Kingdom government arrangement."

A: The Bible Teaches...

Jesus Is God

Jesus is the one true God who "is the same, yesterday, today and forever" (Heb. 13:8; Rev. 1:7–8). Coming to earth, Jesus added human nature to his divine person and is forever the God-Man (Acts 17:31; 1 Tim. 2:5). He never ceased being God (Phil. 2:5–11), nor did he cease being human when he rose from the dead (Luke 24:39; John 2:19–22). One day "every eye will see him" physically return to earth (Rev. 1:7; Matt. 24:30) in the same manner that he visibly ascended into heaven (Acts 1:9–11).

Jesus Isn't Michael

The Watchtower's attempts to link Michael and Jesus are not supported by scripture; the verses used never clearly identify Jesus as Michael the Archangel. Hebrews 1 and 2 present Jesus as greater than the angels. Jude 9 states that Michael the Archangel did not have authority to rebuke Satan, yet Jesus did on a number of occasions (for example, Matt. 16:23).

The Archangel Michael, mosaic

You Should Also Know...

The Only True God

Does Satan's title "god of this world" prove that Jesus is "a god" like Satan? No! Paul clarifies the matter about other "gods" mentioned in Scripture when he declares that "even if there are so-called gods whether in heaven or on earth, as indeed there are many gods and many lords, yet for us there is *but* one God, the Father … and one Lord, Jesus Christ" (1 Cor. 8:5–6). Since there is only one true God, all other "so-called gods" fall under the "false god" category. The Bible calls Satan "god of this world" because the deceived world worships him as such, but he is a false "god" and can save no one. In the same way, Jesus is either the one true God or he is a false "god."

"And we are in him who is true, in his Son Jesus Christ. This is the true God and eternal life" (1 John 5:20).

"For in him [Jesus] all the fullness of Deity dwells in bodily form" (Col. 2:9).

5. Is the Holy Spirit Just God's "Active Force"?

The Watchtower Claims...

An "Active Force"
The holy spirit is an impersonal "active force" which emanates from Jehovah to perform assorted supernatural operations. Since the holy spirit is said to "dwell" within believers, it never appears as a person in Scripture.

The Bible Teaches...

A Real Person
Throughout Scripture, qualities of personhood are attributed to the Holy Spirit. He is seen as one who testifies (John 15:26), intercedes (Rom. 8:26), teaches (John 14:26), and guides believers (Rom. 8:14). He has a mind (Rom. 8:27) and a will (1 Cor. 12:11). He can be grieved (Eph. 4:30), lied to (Acts 5:3), blasphemed (Matt. 12:31), and tested (Acts 5:9). Just as demon spirits of Jesus' day retained their personhood while entering in and dwelling within people (Luke 8:27–30), so the Holy Spirit is no less a person because he can dwell within believers (Eph. 5:18).

Personification or Personhood?
When faced with verses that attribute personality to the Holy Spirit, Jehovah's Witnesses explain them by claiming that they are merely "personifications" of abstract qualities like wisdom, which is personified in the book of Proverbs. However, wisdom is personified in highly poetic passages in Proverbs, whereas the Holy Spirit is attributed personality in various non-poetic contexts (historical narratives, sermons, and epistles). There is simply no comparison between the personification of inanimate objects or abstract qualities in Scripture and the attributions of personal characteristics to the Holy Spirit.

You Should Also Know...

The Holy Spirit Is God
Since Jehovah's Witnesses view the Holy Spirit as an impersonal force, they also deny that he is God. But in Acts 5:3–4, Scripture proclaims the Holy Spirit is God when Ananias lies to the Holy Spirit and is told, "You have not lied to men but to God." Second Corinthians 3:17 declares that "the Lord is the Spirit." Acts 28:25–27 reveals the Holy Spirit as the Lord God of Isaiah 6:8–10.

The Spirit Taken Away?
Scripture proclaims that the Holy Spirit leads "all" who are adopted as children of God (Rom. 8:14–15). Today, most Jehovah's Witnesses would be surprised to learn that on pages 216–217 of the 1939 Watchtower book *Salvation,* the Society proclaimed that "In the year 1918 ... the holy spirit that had been the guide of God's people, having performed its function, was taken away." The Watchtower no longer teaches that the Holy Spirit has left the earth, but they now claim that only people who make up a special group of 144,000 are able to be "spirit anointed" and adopted into God's family.

6 Q. Will Only 144,000 People Go to Heaven?

The Watchtower Claims...

Two Classes of Christians

The 144,000 Christians who were living between Pentecost (c. AD 30) and 1935, called the "anointed class" or "little flock," will live in heaven as spirits forever. Virtually everyone who became a Jehovah's Witnesses after 1935, along with those who never heard of Christ from all ages but were not wicked, are the "other sheep" and will have a chance to live forever as human beings in a paradise on earth. The earthly class will never see God or Jesus Christ. These two classes will remain eternally separated.

New Covenant Privileges Only for the 144,000

Only members of the heavenly class are parties to the new covenant. They alone have Jesus as their mediator, are "born again," have "adoption" as God's children, are members of the "Christian congregation" (the church), may partake of the "memorial emblems" of Jesus' last supper once a year, and will rule from heaven over the earth.

The Bible Teaches...

All Believers Will Live Together in the New Heaven and New Earth

When believers in Christ die they go immediately into Christ's presence (Luke 23:43; Phil. 1:21–24). All believers from all ages will be resurrected with immortal human bodies like Christ's (Rom. 8:11; 1 Cor. 15:42–54; Phil. 3:21) and live together in the New Heaven and New Earth (Matt. 5:5; 2 Pet. 3:13; Rev. 21:1). Believers in Christ will "reign on the earth" (Rev. 5:10). (This "reign" may refer to God's intention for people to exercise dominion on earth [Gen. 1:26, 28], or to Christians ruling over the redeemed from past ages.) All of the redeemed will see God and Christ (Matt. 5:8; 1 John 3:2; Rev. 21:3–4).

All Believers Are in the New Covenant

Christ is the mediator between God and all people who are redeemed in him (1 Tim. 2:5–6). Everyone who has faith in Christ is already "born again" (1 Pet. 1:3; 1 John 5:1). Everyone who knows God as Father through Jesus Christ has the "adoption as sons" (Rom. 8:14–17; Gal. 4:4–6) and are God's children (John 1:12–13). All baptized believers are part of the church, the body of Christ (1 Cor. 12:13).

You Should Also Know...

Who Are the 144,000?

The only two Bible references to 144,000 are in Revelation 7 and 14. Christians who take the number literally also take the twelve Israelite tribes of 12,000 literally (Rev. 7:4–8). It makes no sense to take the number 144,000 literally but not the twelve groups of 12,000 that the text adds up to get 144,000. Christians who take the twelve tribes in this passage as symbolizing the church consistently regard the number 144,000 as symbolic. There is no basis in Revelation 7 or any other passage for dividing Christians into two classes.

Can Only Jehovah's Witnesses Be Saved?

The Watchtower Claims...

Salvation Requirements

Jesus died as a "ransom sacrifice" to buy back what Adam lost: the right to perfect life on earth. Most Witnesses hope to be found worthy enough to be "saved" from destruction in the future battle of Armageddon and to survive into God's new earthly system of rule, when "paradise" will be restored to earth. The four requirements for salvation are: (1) taking in knowledge of Jehovah God and of Jesus Christ; (2) obeying God's laws and conforming one's life to the moral requirements set out in the Bible; (3) belonging to and serving with God's one true channel and organization (that is, the Watchtower Society); and (4) being loyal to God's organization.

No Assurance

Salvation is earned through a combination of faith plus good works. True Christians can have no assurance of eternal life. They must work toward perfection throughout this life, and then throughout Christ's 1,000-year reign on earth. Next they must pass the final test of Satan (during which Satan is released from the pit to tempt all faithful Witnesses one last time) before God will grant them eternal life. If they fail at any point they are at risk of annihilation (eternal destruction).

The Bible Teaches...

Good Works Can't Save

The Bible declares that "all our righteous deeds are like a filthy garment" (Isa. 64:6) and that "There is none righteous.... for all have sinned and fall short of the glory of God" (Rom. 3:10, 23). To be saved one must come to Jesus empty-handed, offering one's sin in exchange for his righteousness (Phil. 3:9; 2 Cor. 5:21; Eph. 2:8–9). Good works are the fruit (evidence), not the root (cause), of a saved relationship with God (Mark 4:20; Eph. 2:10).

Full Assurance

No one can earn or deserve salvation; it is a "free gift" from God based on Christ's merit, not human worthiness (Rom. 6:23). Those who "have the Son" have the full assurance of eternal life (1 John 5:10-13). Thus, only because of Jesus, true Christians will rise from death, made perfect in Christ (Heb. 10:10, 14; John 5:24).

You Should Also Know...

Only Two Destinies

Contrary to Watchtower thinking, there will be no 1,000-year period for people who have died to be given a second chance at perfection. Revelation 20:5 states that those who are not part of the first resurrection will "not come to life until the thousand years" are completed. Only those whose names are written in the Lamb's Book of Life will be admitted to heaven, while the rest of the dead will be condemned to the "lake of fire" (Rev. 20:15). After the final judgment, God will bring about the New Heaven and New Earth with no trace of sin's curse (2 Pet. 3:7, 10–13; Heb.1:10–12; Rev. 21).

Watchtower magazine, August 15, 1997

8 Q. Is the Watchtower's *New World Translation* Reliable?

The Watchtower Claims...

Humble, Honest Translators

The *New World Translation* (NWT) is the official Bible of the Watchtower Society. It is the most accurate, unbiased Bible version available today. The translators remain anonymous so that all glory for the translation will go to Jehovah God.

Other, Distorted Translations

Referring to other English translations, the 1950 NWT states that "while each of them has its points of merit, they have fallen victim to the power of human traditions. …[I]nconsistency and unreasonableness have been insinuated into the teachings of the inspired writings." By contrast, "The endeavor of the New World Bible Translation Committee has been to avoid this snare of religious traditionalism." In 1969, the Watchtower published *The Kingdom Interlinear Translation of the Greek Scriptures* (KIT), "a literal word-for-word translation into English under the Greek text." The foreword claims that by using the KIT "the accuracy of any modern translation can be determined."

A. The Bible Teaches...

Jesus Christ Is God

The Bible's teaching that Jesus Christ is God is obscured in the NWT, as may be seen by comparing the NWT with the Greek-English text of the Watchtower's own KIT:

John 8:58: "Before Abraham came into existence, I **have been**" (NWT)/ "Before Abraham to become I **am**" (KIT)

John 14:14: "If you ask anything..." (NWT) / "If ever anything you should ask **me**..." (KIT)

Colossians 1:16–17: Christ created "all **[other]** things" (NWT) / Christ created "all (things)" (KIT)

Colossians 2:9: "all the fullness of **divine quality**" dwells in Christ (NWT) / "all the fullness of **the divinity**" dwells in Christ (KIT)

You Should Also Know...

Translators Identified

The NWT translation committee was composed of six men, five of whom had no formal training in biblical languages. Frederick Franz, the head of the committee, was a knowledgeable amateur.

More Mistranslations

The NWT contains numerous examples of doctrinally biased renderings, including these:

Matthew 25:46: "And these will depart into everlasting **cutting-off**," rather than "punishment," because Witnesses don't believe the wicked will be punished forever.

Luke 23:43: "Truly I tell you **today**, You will be with me in Paradise." The NWT has the comma after "today" because Witnesses don't believe human beings exist as spirits after death. (Jesus' frequent use of "Truly I tell you" makes it certain that "today" goes with what follows.)

1 Corinthians 15:44: "It is sown a **physical** body" (1 Cor. 15:44), instead of "natural," because Witnesses believe that Jesus was not raised in a physical body. (The same word is used in 1 Cor. 2:14, where the NWT also incorrectly has "physical.")

1 Timothy 4:1: "However, **the inspired utterance** says," instead of "the Spirit," because Witnesses don't believe that the Holy Spirit is a person.

Which Is the Final Authority: The Bible or the Watchtower?

The Watchtower Claims...

God's "Channel"
Throughout history, beginning with the nation of Israel, God has always led his people through a visible organization. When Israel refused to accept Jesus as the Messiah, God ordained a new, prophetic "channel of communication": the Christian congregation (that is, the church). After Christendom became apostate, God fulfilled Jesus' prophecy in Matthew 24:45-47 that a "faithful and discreet slave" would dispense "spiritual food" to Jehovah's people in the last days. The Watchtower Society fulfills this passage through its worldwide teaching and publishing program.

No "Independent Thinking"
Spiritual truth is not given to God's people individually, but only through his ordained channel (the Watchtower). Thus, Jehovah's Witnesses must accept the Watchtower's interpretation of Scripture over their personal ideas and analyses; "independent thinking" is dangerous. Any Witness who challenges the Watchtower's current doctrines may be labeled prideful and "spiritually weak" and be subject to shunning by other Witnesses.

The Bible Teaches...

Truth Is a Person, Not an Organization
The Bible proclaims Jesus is the *only* mediator between God and man (1 Tim. 2:5). In the Old Testament people were required to approach God through sacrifices by the Israelite priestly organization; later, Jesus became the final sacrifice ending the separation between man and God caused by sin. Since Jesus is our ultimate High Priest (Heb. 6:20; 7:24), we no longer need an earthly organization to go to God. Jesus said, "I am the way, and the truth, and the life; no one comes to the Father, but through me" (John 14:6).

Test All Things
The New Testament commends the Christians in Berea (Greece) for being "more noble-minded" because they tested Paul's message by Scripture (Acts 17:10–11). In 1 Thessalonians 5:19–22 Christians are encouraged to question prophetic claims ("examine everything carefully") and reject what is false ("abstain from every form of evil"), a pattern begun in the Old Testament (for instance, Deut. 18:21–22).

You Should Also Know...

The Real "Slave"
In Matthew 24:45–51 Jesus uses the example of a faithful slave whose master returns unexpectedly to warn his disciples to be alert for his return. Nowhere does he indicate that the parable applies only to an organization; rather, it is given to individual Christians. When Christ returns, everyone who is faithful will be rewarded by reigning with him, while those who neglect their duties will be punished (as is the unfaithful slave in this story).

A Record of False Prophecy
Jesus warns his followers of false prophets who falsely announce his return (Matt. 24:23–34). The Watchtower Society fulfills the criteria of a false prophet, having pointed to 1874 as the date when Christ's presence began and currently teaching that it began in 1914. It is guilty of repeatedly predicting the end of the age: 1914, 1915, 1918, 1925, 1940s, and 1975. And while demanding absolute devotion to its teachings and proclaiming that it alone has "the Truth," the Watchtower has reversed itself on a number of doctrines.

10

Q: What Else Do Jehovah's Witnesses Believe?

A:

The Watchtower Claims...

No Blood Transfusions
Transfusing blood into one's veins violates God's law against eating blood in Leviticus 17:14 and Acts 15:29. Even when rejecting a transfusion costs a Jehovah's Witness his life, this helps secure a future place in Paradise.

No Holidays and Celebrations
Birthday and holiday celebrations have pagan origins. Jesus only commanded the celebration of his death, so true Christians do not commemorate anything but Jesus' death (and their own wedding anniversaries).

No Politics or War
Because they have "no part" in the "wicked system" of this world, true Christians do not involve themselves in politics, vote in elections, salute national flags, or fight in war.

The Bible Teaches...

Eating, Not Transfusing
The Old Testament injunction was against the eating of blood; transfused blood is neither digested nor metabolized by the body when it enters through the veins.

Birthdays and Holidays Celebrated
The memorial of Jesus' death was not the only event Jesus' followers observed. Since they were Jews, they likely observed all the Jewish holidays, just as they did Hanukkah (John 10:22). Watchtower objections to celebrations based on pagan origins can be answered by the fact that many customs today have lost their pagan significance. So, the principle of Christian freedom Paul gives in Romans 14 when addressing the subject of holiday celebrations and eating pagan sacrificial meat should hold true for all Christians. In verses 5 and 6 he writes, "Let each man be fully convinced in his own mind. He who observes the day, observes it for the Lord, and he who eats, does so for the Lord."

You Should Also Know...

Christians in World Governments
At Matthew 5:13–16, Scripture encourages Christians to function as "salt" and "light" in their communities. This included prominent Bible characters who were both militarily and politically active. Daniel and his colleagues were high-ranking officials in the pagan government of Babylon. The Ethiopian eunuch in Acts 8 was in charge of the treasury. Jesus commends the centurion (captain of 100 soldiers) for his "great faith" in Matthew 8, and the soldier Cornelius is also commended as a "God-fearing man" in Acts 10. Paul mentions a Christian named Erastus, the city treasurer, which was a politically appointed government job (Rom. 16:23).

Jehovah's Witnesses and Medicine
In addition to its changing positions on blood transfusions, the Watchtower Society has taken dogmatic and controversial medical stands which it later reversed. For decades, Watchtower publications condemned both pasteurization and the germ theory of disease, and campaigned vigorously against aluminum cooking utensils (calling them "a curse to humanity"). In years past the Society has forbidden its followers to accept vaccinations ("a crime against nature") and organ transplants ("cannibalism").

Tips for Talking with Jehovah's Witnesses

Do pray before each encounter with the Jehovah's Witnesses and invite the Holy Spirit to lead and guide the conversation. Ask that he would fill their minds and hearts with the Truth of his Word.

Don't depend on evidence and argumentation alone. Rely on the Holy Spirit to guide you. It is the Holy Spirit's job to convict of sin, righteousness and judgment.

Do approach Jehovah's Witnesses in a humble, loving attitude. Identify with them in genuine concern and treat them respectfully, realizing they probably would not have joined had they known all the facts.

Don't approach them with a superior attitude, belittle them, or act like you have something they don't.

Do ask the Jehovah's Witness to help you understand how to reconcile their beliefs with the Bible. Jehovah's Witnesses are trained to teach, not to listen to you. Questions can be a powerful tool to break through their programmed responses and to get them to "think" for themselves.

Don't confront Jehovah's Witnesses in an argumentative manner, trying to "teach" them. Jehovah's Witnesses believe they have "the Truth" and that you don't have anything to offer them.

Do challenge the Jehovah's Witnesses' trust in the Watchtower by showing discrepancies in their own literature. Jehovah's Witnesses are not allowed to read anti-Watchtower literature, so use their literature and Scripture alone.

Don't engage in deep scriptural discussion too soon. Witnesses are told they can't understand the Bible apart from Watchtower literature, so their trust in the Watchtower needs to be broken before they can begin to interpret the Bible for themselves.

Do pray to "Jehovah God" with Jehovah's Witnesses and pray about personal things that are happening in their lives. Emphasize the "Father" aspect of "Jehovah" in your prayer and how he cares for you personally.

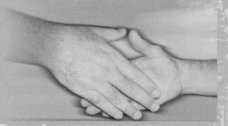

Don't pray to "God" or "Lord" without addressing the prayer to "Jehovah" at some point. Jehovah's Witnesses fear that if a prayer doesn't have Jehovah's name, it may end up in Satan's hands. Also, don't ask if you can pray with them for healing of sickness (unless they approach you privately). They're taught that God doesn't "heal" today and anything miraculous is done by Satan to deceive the unsuspecting.

Do tell Jehovah's Witnesses about your personal relationship with Jesus and how he answers prayer and personally works in your life. Jehovah's Witnesses do not believe God cares as much for them as he does for the organization, so your testimony can make them hungry for a real relationship with the true God.

Don't try to force the Jehovah's Witness to "agree" with you. They're not allowed to disagree with the Watchtower, so plant seeds of doubt through your questions and let the Holy Spirit do his work.

Do be available, persistent and patient. If they're asking questions, they're starting to think for themselves. This is the first step to leaving the Watchtower.

Names: Watchtower Bible and Tract Society; International Bible Students Association

Year/Place Founded: 1879 (incorporated 1884); Pittsburgh, Pennsylvania (USA)

Founder: Charles Taze Russell (1852–1916)

World Headquarters: Brooklyn, New York (USA)

Estimated Adherents: 19 million in over 235 nations and territories (2012)

Materials: Publishes magazines, books, and other materials in over 500 languages (2012)

Quick Facts

Terms and Definitions

Adventists: Followers of the various movements inspired by the teachings of American preacher William Miller (1782–1849), who predicted that the Second Coming of Christ would take place in 1843 or 1844.

Anointed Class: The special people who are "anointed" with God's Spirit, said to number 144,000; the only people going to heaven according to Watchtower theology.

Apostasy: In general use, a falling away from one's faith. For Jehovah's Witnesses, a turning away from God by leaving His organization, the Watchtower Bible and Tract Society. Jehovah's Witnesses are forbidden to read "apostate" literature (literature critical of the Watchtower) or personal letters from "apostates" (people who have left the Watchtower).

Armageddon: The final battle between wicked mankind and Jehovah God to end world governments and bring about the establishment of Jehovah's Kingdom rule on Paradise Earth.

Assembly: A large gathering of Jehovah's Witnesses for Watchtower conventions.

Babylon: All non-Jehovah's Witness religious organizations and worldly governments.

Bible Study: One-on-one home studies, using Watchtower literature, designed to recruit new people into the organization.

Christendom: Disparaging term used to describe "professed Christianity"—that is, all non-Jehovah's Witness religions that claim to be Christian—in contrast with "the true Christianity of the Bible." Viewed as under Satan's control.

Christian Greek Scriptures: Jehovah's Witness term for "New Testament." The Old Testament is called "Hebrew Scriptures."

Disassociate, Disfellowship: Terms applied to a Jehovah's Witness who formally leaves the Watchtower organization of his own volition (disassociates) or is expelled from the Watchtower (disfellowshipped). In either case, active Jehovah's Witnesses consider the one leaving an "apostate" and therefore subject to "shunning."

Earthly Class: People who followed Jehovah God and lived on earth prior to Pentecost in AD 33 or became Jehovah's Witnesses after 1935; their eternal destiny according to the Watchtower is everlasting life on Paradise earth.

Faithful and Discreet Slave: The servant commended in Jesus' story in Matthew 24:45 who proved faithful in caring for his master's provisions and was granted oversight of all his master's belongings upon his return. The Watchtower applies the parable to its "Governing Body" leadership and claims that it alone has been granted spiritual authority over Jehovah's people.

Great Crowd: Group of people mentioned in Revelation whose number no one can count (Revelation 7:9). In the Watchtower's interpretation these people are an "earthly class" relegated to live eternally on the earth.

Heavenly Class: Another name for the "Anointed Class."

Kingdom Hall: Building for weekly meetings of two to three local congregations of Jehovah's Witnesses. (The word "church" is never used to refer to Watchtower meeting places.)

Little Flock: Another name for the "Anointed Class", based on a misreading of Luke 12:32. (Jesus was simply referring to the small size of his band of followers at the time.)

Other Sheep: Another name for the "Earthly class", drawn from John 10:16. (By "other sheep" Jesus meant Gentiles who would come to faith in him.)

Overseer: An elder assigned to oversee specific responsibilities within the congregation or larger Jehovah's Witness gatherings.

New Light: Watchtower euphemism for changes in doctrine.

New World: Paradise Earth, where only faithful Jehovah's Witnesses who survived Armageddon will reside.

Paradise: Nature on earth restored to pre-curse conditions, the Garden of Eden in Genesis.

Pioneer: A Jehovah's Witness who participates full-time in the door-to-door "Preaching Work" for a set number of hours per month.

Preaching Work: Door-to-door distribution of Watchtower literature and home Bible studies conducted with potential converts.

Publisher: A baptized or unbaptized Jehovah's Witness who participates in the "preaching work." No set minimum number of hours is required.

Russellites: Nickname given to those who follow the teachings of Watchtower Society founder Charles Taze Russell, especially so-called "Bible Student" groups that reject teachings introduced by the Society after his death.

Shunning: A form of disciplinary exclusion in which "apostate" Jehovah's Witnesses are ignored and treated as if dead by their Witness friends and relatives.

Tetragrammaton: The four Old Testament Hebrew consonants (transliterated into English as "YHWH") from which God's name is derived.

The Truth: Another name for the Watchtower organization's changing doctrines.

Theocracy: God's kingdom rule.

Resources

The inclusion of a work does not necessarily mean endorsement of all its contents or of other works by the same author(s).

LITERATURE

Jehovah's Witnesses by Robert M. Bowman, Jr. (Zondervan, 1995).

Why You Should Believe in the Trinity by Robert M. Bowman, Jr. (Baker Book House, 1989)

Reasoning from the Scriptures with the Jehovah's Witnesses by Ron Rhodes (Harvest House Publishers, 1993)

Jehovah's Witnesses Answered Verse by Verse by David A. Reed (Baker Book House, 1986).

How to Rescue Your Loved One from the Watchtower by David A. Reed (Baker Book House, 1989)

Crisis of Conscience by Raymond Franz (Commentary Press, 2002)

What Does God Require? Biblical Answers to Questions Jehovah's Witnesses Ask by Christy (Harvey) Darlington (Witnesses for Jesus, 2001)

Jehovah's Witnesses: Their Claims, Doctrinal Changes, and Prophetic Speculation. What Does the Record Show? by Edmond C. Gruss (Xulon Press, 2001)

VIDEO/DVD

In the Name of Jehovah (North American Mission Board, 2004)

Witnesses of Jehovah (Good News Defenders, 1988)

The Witness at Your Door and *The Witness Goes Out!* (Jeremiah Films, 1992)

Battling Over the Children (Jeremiah Films, 1994)

Jehovah's Witnesses and the Real Jesus (MMOutreach, 1995)

POWERPOINT®

10 Questions & Answers on Jehovah's Witnesses (Rose Publishing, Inc., 2006)

INTERNET

Witnesses for Jesus, Inc.
www.4witness.org

FreeMinds, Inc.
www.freeminds.org

TowerWatch Ministries
www.towerwatch.com

Let Us Reason Ministries
www.letusreason.org

Facts About Jehovah's Witnesses
www.jwfacts.com

Resources on the *New World Translation*
www.tetragrammaton.org

Silent Lambs
www.silentlambs.org

Watchtower Quotes
http://quotes-watchtower.co.uk

Jehovah's Witnesses and Blood
www.ajwrb.org

Testimonies of Former Jehovah's Witnesses
www.jwinfoline.com/Page/audio.htm

JW Research
www.premier1.net/~raines/index.html

General Editor: Paul Carden, Executive Director, Centers for Apologetics Research (CFAR)
Principal Author: Christy (Harvey) Darlington, President, Witnesses for Jesus, Inc.
Contributor: Robert M. Bowman, Jr., MA in Biblical Studies & Theology

10 Questions & Answers on
Mormonism

Was Joseph Smith a True Prophet of God?

Is the Mormon God the God of the Bible?

Does Mormonism Teach the Truth About Jesus?

Why do Mormons Build Temples?

Q. Did the Christian Church Really Need to Be Restored?

Mormonism Claims...

Complete Apostasy

According to Mormon prophets, after the death of Jesus' original apostles, the Christian church gradually slipped into "the Great Apostasy"—a complete and universal abandonment of true Christian principles. Though we do not know exactly when this took place, Christian doctrine became thoroughly corrupted, and the priesthood authority necessary to administer key ordinances like baptism and the Lord's Supper was lost. The importance of believing that the true church was destroyed is underscored by Mormon apostle James Talmage: "If the alleged apostasy of the primitive Church was not a reality, The Church of Jesus Christ of Latter-day Saints is not the divine institution its name proclaims."[1]

Restoration Required

The restoration of true Christianity began when God the Father and Jesus Christ appeared to a youth named Joseph Smith in the spring of 1820. In this "First Vision" Jesus told Smith that all the churches were wrong and that all their creeds (statements of belief) were "an abomination."[2] God used Smith to organize his true church again in 1830.

A. The Bible Teaches...

No General Apostasy

Jesus promised his followers that he would be with them in their ministry of making disciples, baptizing, and teaching, "even unto the end of the world" (Matt. 28:20). He promised that he would build his church, and that the "gates of hell shall not prevail against it" (Matt. 16:18). Such promises would have been broken had Jesus allowed his church to be "destroyed." While the Bible does mention that "some" shall depart from the faith (1 Tim. 4:1), it never implies that a universal or "complete" apostasy would take place prior to his return. The fact that "some [would] depart" implies that others would not. The New Testament here and elsewhere portrays apostasy as the acts and attitudes of individuals and groups breaking away from the church (see also 1 John 2:19), not as the church ceasing to exist.

Joseph Smith's "First Vision"
Stained glass window at the Museum of Church History and Art in Salt Lake City, Utah

You Should Also Know...

Though the Latter-day Saints (LDS) church views the many Christian denominations as proof that Christ's "One True Church" was lost, numerous LDS splinter groups exist. The second largest of these groups is the Community of Christ (known originally as the Reorganized Church of Jesus Christ of Latter Day Saints, or RLDS). Additionally, numerous "fundamentalist" LDS groups believe that the Utah-based LDS church itself became apostate when it officially renounced polygamy in 1890.

Was Joseph Smith a True Prophet of God?

Mormonism Claims...

Uniquely Important

Joseph Smith (1805–1844), the church's founder and first president, is a modern "prophet, seer, and revelator" (a person who reveals divine truth). He is ranked in importance second only to Jesus Himself when it comes to the salvation of mankind: "Joseph Smith, the Prophet and Seer of the Lord, has done more, save Jesus only, for the salvation of men in this world, than any other man that ever lived in it."[3] Many believe that the most convincing witness to Joseph's calling as a prophet is the Book of Mormon, which he called "the most correct of any book on earth."[4]

Genuine or Fraud

According to tenth LDS president Joseph Fielding Smith, "Mormonism, as it is called, must stand or fall on the story of Joseph Smith. He was either a prophet of God, divinely called, properly appointed and commissioned, or he was one of the biggest frauds this world has ever seen. There is no middle ground."[5]

The Bible Teaches...

Testing Prophets

God provided two main tests for Israelites to determine whether a self-proclaimed prophet was legitimate. First, he must represent the true God of the Hebrews; prophets who introduced false gods were to be immediately rejected (Deut. 13:1–3). Second, they were to reject professing prophets who incorrectly foretold the future (Deut. 18:20–22). They were also commanded not to add to or take away from the revelations God had given them (Deut. 4:2; Prov. 30:6).

Joseph Smith receives the Book of Mormon from Moroni
© Bill McKeever. Used with permission.

You Should Also Know...

Joseph Smith denied the biblical view of God (see Question 6). He falsely predicted that a war between the States would literally become a world war.[6] And although the Bible warns against adding or taking away from what God has commanded, Joseph Smith produced his own version of the Bible in which he took out some parts and inserted others (see Question 3).

Mormon leaders have often made incredible statements about the role and character of Joseph Smith.

For example, Mormon prophet Brigham Young and his counselor, George Q. Cannon, both insisted that the only way a Latter-day Saint could hope to enter the highest level of Mormon heaven (the celestial kingdom) was if he had Joseph Smith's permission.[7] Mormon apostle Bruce McConkie also declared that "all men in the latter days must turn to Joseph Smith to gain salvation,"[8] and that Joseph Smith aided God the Father in the creation of the earth.[9]

Q. What Is Mormon Scripture?

Mormonism Claims...

Four "Standard Works"
The LDS church accepts four books as its "standard works":
- The Bible (King James Version)
- The Book of Mormon—a translation of an ancient document that gives an account of three people groups who migrated to the Americas from the Middle East, the latest of these arriving about 589 BC.
- The Doctrine and Covenants—a collection of modern revelations, most of which were given by LDS church founder Joseph Smith.
- The Pearl of Great Price—a collection of smaller works.

Of these four, only the Bible is considered to have corruptions and is accepted with qualifications (*see Question 4*).

Continuing Revelation
Mormons are also instructed to accept the words of their living prophets. Because of their belief in continuing revelation, Mormons do not view their scriptures as being "closed," meaning that some doctrines may be changed or added in the future.

A. The Bible Teaches...

The Bible vs. Mormon Revelations
The Bible says it's a serious offense to claim God said something when he actually didn't. Before Mormon scripture can be given any credibility at all it must agree with what God has *already* revealed in the Bible— for example, see Acts 17:11, Hebrews 1:1–2. (The Mormon church takes no such position. In fact, the church's First Presidency has insisted that the "most reliable way to measure the accuracy of any biblical passage is not by comparing different texts, but by comparison with the Book of Mormon and modern-day revelations.")[10]

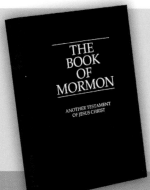

You Should Also Know...

Doctrine and Covenants 73:4 states that God commanded Joseph Smith to finish a new translation of the Bible. On July 2, 1833, Smith wrote, "We this day finished the translating of the Scriptures...."[11] To call his new Bible a "translation" is very misleading since this Bible, known as the *Inspired Version* or *Joseph Smith Translation* (JST), wasn't really a translation at all. Smith had no ancient manuscripts in his possession, nor was he fluent in any biblical language. Rather than consult ancient texts, Joseph merely opened his Bible and "corrected" whatever he felt was necessary according to his view at the time (for example, adding a prophecy of his own birth to Gen. 50:33). Though the Mormon church does not publish its own bound version of Smith's complete Bible, it does include Smith's alterations in footnotes and endnotes of its edition of the King James Version.

Q: Is the Bible Trustworthy Scripture?

Mormonism Claims...

Unreliable Scripture

The LDS church affirms that "We believe the Bible to be the word of God as far as it is translated correctly."[12] The church's First Presidency also cautions that "The Bible, as it has been transmitted over the centuries, has suffered the loss of many plain and precious parts."[13] Thus, latter-day revelation from the Mormon church's living prophets always takes precedence over the ancient written word.

As Mormon apostle Orson Pratt asked, "... who in his right mind could for one moment suppose the Bible in its present form to be a perfect guide? Who knows that even one verse of the Bible has escaped pollution, so as to convey the same sense now that it did in the original?" [14]

A: The Bible Teaches...

Reliable Revelations

"All Scripture is God-breathed and useful for teaching, rebuking, correcting, and training in righteousness" (2 Tim. 3:16). It has been correctly argued that when Paul refers to "scripture" here he means the Old Testament. However, Paul appears to quote the Gospel of Luke as Scripture (1 Tim. 5:18, citing Luke 10:7), and Peter explicitly refers to Paul's writings as Scripture as well (2 Pet. 3:16).

God's Word stands forever and will not fail to accomplish his purpose (Isa. 40:8; 55:11; see also Matt. 24:35). These passages indicate that God has guaranteed that his Word in Scripture would be preserved sufficiently to accurately convey his revealed truth.

Bust of past President Gordon B. Hinckley *in the Conference Center Hall of the Prophets in Salt Lake City, Utah*

You Should Also Know...

LDS criticisms of the Bible typically have more to do with allegations of faulty "transmission" (the copying of the original texts in the same language) than with faulty translation. Mormons are given the impression that the Bible has been extensively revised by corrupt transcribers and religious leaders who either removed important ideas or inserted false teaching. As a result, many Mormons do not feel compelled to reexamine their beliefs when Bible passages contradict what their leaders have told them.

While original documents by the hands of biblical authors no longer exist, critical examination of the thousands of available manuscript copies allows us to determine with great accuracy precisely what the original writers wrote. Although no two ancient manuscripts of the Bible read exactly the same, the differences (called "variants") are essentially minor and do not support radically different religious ideas—such as the Mormon belief that God the Father was once a man.

Is the Book of Mormon an Ancient Document?

Mormonism Claims...

Miraculous Translation

The Book of Mormon is a miraculous translation of an ancient document. By "the gift and power of God," Joseph Smith interpreted the "reformed Egyptian" characters on the golden plates that the angel Moroni gave him in 1827.

The Book of Mormon gives an account of three people groups (the Lehites, Jaredites, and Mulekites) who migrated from the Middle East and inhabited the American continents "between about 2000 BC and AD 400."[15]

Biblical Prophecy

The coming forth of the Book of Mormon was foretold centuries ago in Ezekiel 37:16–17, in which the "sticks" described are actually two books: the Bible and the Book of Mormon.

The Bible Teaches...

Nations—Not Books

The Hebrew word for "stick" in Ezekiel 37 is never used in connection with books and is consistently translated as a literal stick, a branch, or some other wood product (see Num. 15:32, 33; 1 Kings 17:12; 2 Kings 6:6). In Ezekiel 37, the prophet himself explains that the sticks represent two *nations*: the ten northern tribes of Israel and the two southern tribes of Judah. Israel and Judah had been separated since the reign of King Rehoboam, and each kingdom had its own set of kings. Ezekiel was predicting that God would one day make them a single nation ruled by one king.

Mormons regard American Indians as descendents of the Lamanites. *Photo by Edward S. Curtis*

You Should Also Know...

Unlike many editions of the Bible, the Book of Mormon is published with no maps. In fact, the LDS church cannot locate even one unique Book of Mormon city, and it has failed to provide undisputed proof that the peoples it describes (such as Nephites) really existed. Despite the claim that the Book of Mormon is an ancient document, its 19th-century origin is exposed by the way it quotes and paraphrases passages from the New Testament (for example, compare Matt. 19:30 with 1 Nephi 13:42;

John 12:40 with 1 Nephi 13:27). It also mentions topics relating to freemasonry and doctrinal controversies (such as infant baptism) that were hotly disputed during Smith's lifetime.

The Book of Mormon mentions types of animals, weaponry, and plants which were not present in the New World during the Book of Mormon time period. New DNA research undermines the Mormon claim that the "Lamanites" (described as the "principal ancestors of the American Indians") are actually of Semitic origin.

Is the God of Mormonism the God of the Bible?

Mormonism Claims...

Many Gods

The one whom Christians call "Our Heavenly Father" is one God among many Gods stretching into eternity past. This same God was at one time a mortal, finite human who attained his current exalted (deified) state by obedience to eternal laws and principles. Joseph Smith proclaimed, "We have imagined and supposed that God was God from all eternity. I will refute that idea, and will take away and do away the veil, so that you may see."[16]

We Can Become Gods

Fifth LDS president Lorenzo Snow stated, "As man is, God once was; as God is, man may become."[17] God the Father has "a body of flesh and bones as tangible as man's"[18] and can only be at one place at any one time. The view of God held by millions of Christians is a perversion of the truth.

In the words of Mormon apostle Orson Pratt, "If we should take a million of worlds like this and number their particles, we should find that there are more Gods than there are particles of matter in those worlds."[19]

The Bible Teaches...

Only One Eternal God

God has always been eternally God (Ps. 90:2), and he is responsible for all things created (John 1:3). God is spirit (John 4:24), and one does well to believe that there is only one God (James 2:19). The Bible declares that the Father is God, the Son is God, and the Holy Spirit is God (Rom. 1:7; John 20:28; Acts 5:3–4), yet it also proclaims firmly that God is one (Deut. 6:4) while making a clear distinction among the persons. The God of the Bible is all-knowing (omniscient), yet he declares that he knows of no other gods (Isa. 44:8). God insists that before him no god was formed, neither shall there be any god that comes after him (Isa. 43:10; 44:6). The Apostle Paul noted the foolishness of those who change the glory of the incorruptible God into an image like that of corruptible man (Rom. 1:22–23). In brief, the God described in the Bible is not the God in which Mormons believe.

You Should Also Know...

Christianity has always declared that the God of the Bible is the primary cause of all things; He is the *uncaused cause*. LDS church leaders often speak of *eternal laws*, but it is inconceivable that the God worshiped by Mormons is responsible for these laws since, according to Joseph Smith, God was not eternally God. Though Mormonism teaches that men have the ability to become Gods, it insists that Mormons who achieve godhood will never become more powerful than the God over this world currently is or will be. Since Mormons teach that each Mormon male has the potential of becoming deity, this allows for the possibility of literally millions of Gods.

All-seeing eye (symbol for God) on Mormon temple in Salt Lake City. *From www.hismin.com. Used by permission.*

7 Q: Does Mormonism Teach the Truth About Jesus?

Mormonism Claims...

Jesus "Preexisted" with Us

Jesus preexisted in heaven before he became a man, died on the cross, rose bodily from the dead, and ascended into heaven. However, *all* human beings preexisted in heaven before becoming human; Jesus is the firstborn of God's spirit children and the first (of many) to have become a God. Although Jesus is a member of the "Godhead," one should not pray to Jesus. As a human being, he is the *literal* son of God the Father through a physical union: "Jesus is the only person on earth to be born of a mortal mother and an immortal father.[20] By his death and resurrection, Jesus secured "immortality" for all human beings— whether they believe in him or not. After he rose from the dead, Jesus went to the Americas to preach to the Nephites there.[21]

Mormon statue of Jesus in Salt Lake City
© Bill McKeever. Used with permission.

A: The Bible Teaches...

One of a Kind

Jesus Christ is *not* the first of God's billions of preexistent spirit children; instead, he is the *only* human being to have preexisted as a spirit in heaven. Speaking of Jesus, John the Baptist said that "he who is of the earth is from the earth and speaks of the earth. He who comes from heaven is above all" (John 3:31). Jesus is from heaven; we are not. As God, Jesus is addressed properly in prayer (John 14:14; Acts 1:24; 7:59–60; 2 Cor. 12:8–9). He was not born as God's literal earthly son by a sexual union, but was conceived by the Holy Spirit (Matt. 1:18; Luke 1:35). By his death and resurrection, Jesus secured resurrection to eternal life only for those whom God redeems through faith (1 Cor. 15; *see Question 8*). There will also be a resurrection of the wicked to face eternal condemnation (Dan. 12:2; John 5:29; Acts 24:15). Since Jesus ascended to heaven, he has been and will remain there until his return in glory (Acts 1:9–11, 3:19–21). Therefore, he did not go to the Americas to preach there.

You Should Also Know...

Mormons believe that God the Father, Jesus Christ, and the Holy Ghost are three Gods, though united in *purpose* as the one "Godhead." This is not the same as the Christian doctrine of the Trinity, in which there is only one true God (Deut. 6:4) existing eternally in the three persons of the Father, Son, and Holy Spirit. Mormons also believe that in addition to a Heavenly Father, all humans and spirits have a Heavenly Mother—despite the fact that there is no mention of her in the Bible or any Mormon scripture.

8. Can We Earn Our Salvation?

Mormonism Claims...

Immortality for All

Salvation by grace alone ("immortality") enables humans to be resurrected from the dead. However, a life of obedience to God's commandments is necessary to have one's sins forgiven and receive "eternal life"—exaltation (and godhood)—in the celestial kingdom where God the Father dwells.

Eternal Life by Our Efforts

Thomas Monson of the LDS First Presidency stated, "It is the celestial glory which we seek. It is in the presence of God we desire to dwell. It is a forever family in which we want membership. Such blessings must be earned."[22] A person's eternal destination depends on individual efforts here on earth: "Every person will inherit a glory of salvation, which will be the one that he has earned."[23]

You Should Also Know...

The Book of Mormon teaches that the grace of Christ only takes effect after the Latter-day Saint has denied himself "of all ungodliness."[24] Though both biblical Christianity and Mormonism have a

A. The Bible Teaches...

Eternal Life by Grace Through Faith

Because mankind is incapable of meeting the standard of perfection necessary to abide in God's presence (Rom. 3:19–20, 23), God sent his Son, Jesus Christ, to pay the total debt for the believer's sins and mercifully credits to his account Christ's righteousness (Rom. 3:21–28, 5:1–11; 2 Cor. 5:18–21). Jesus' gracious act of atonement was complete and covers all sin (Col. 2:13–14; 1 Jn. 1:9). Salvation is not based on good deeds, but according to the mercy of God (Titus 3:4-5). Believers are justified by faith; it is a gift given by God's grace (Rom. 4:3-8; Eph. 2:8-9). A true, living faith will result in a desire to live a holy, loving life of good works (Eph. 2:10; Gal. 5:6; James 2:14-26), but failure to be absolutely successful at righteous living does not negate the believer's justified status.

concept of repentance, in Mormonism this involves successfully abandoning *all* sin: "...Incomplete repentance never brought complete forgiveness."[25] "Those who receive forgiveness and then repeat the sin are held accountable for their former sins."[26] Sin that is not overcome robs the Mormon of any assurance of reaching the celestial kingdom (eternal life). According to Mormon president Spencer W. Kimball, "Living all the commandments guarantees total forgiveness of sins and assures one of exaltation."[27]

9Q. Why Do Mormons Build Temples?

Mormonism Claims...

Rituals for Both Living and Dead

Unlike chapels where members meet on a weekly basis, Mormon temples are special buildings in which various rites necessary for exaltation are performed. The ritual most often performed is baptism for the dead, whereby a living substitute is baptized on behalf of a deceased person. Joseph Smith claimed: "The greatest responsibility in this world that God has placed upon us is to seek after our dead." Members who neglect this "do so at the peril of their own salvation."[28] Temples are also used for marriage ceremonies binding husband and wife together not only for "time," but also for eternity. "Sealing" ceremonies are performed to unite children with their parents for eternity.

Mormon temple in Hong Kong
© Institute for Religious Research.
Used with permission.

A. The Bible Teaches...

Sacrifices—Not Sealings

The primary function of the temple in ancient Israel was the sacrifice of animals, a ritual that has never been a part of Mormonism. The focus was on repentance and forgiveness. People went into the temple because of their unworthiness, offering sacrifices for their sins. This is the opposite of the earned "worthiness" that Mormons believe is essential for Mormon temple participation (*see Question 8*).

There is no biblical mention of any marriages performed in the temple, let alone baptisms for the dead. (Paul's comment about baptism for the dead in 1 Corinthians 15:29 refers to it as something that "they"—those who were denying the resurrection—do, not something Christians do.)

Jesus told the Samaritan woman that temple worship would one day cease (John 4:21–24). Because Christians as a whole represent the "temple of God" (1 Cor. 3:16), and because Jesus offered Himself as the perfect sacrifice, temple worship is no longer necessary.

You Should Also Know...

Mormons are compelled to promise that they will not speak of what they have learned in the temple "endowment ceremony," even to other "temple Mormons." In the endowment, participants are taught special handshakes (called "tokens"), arm gestures ("signs"), and special phrases ("key words"). Brigham Young taught that after a Mormon departs this life, knowledge of tokens, signs, and key words will be necessary in order to pass the angelic sentinels who guard the way back to the presence of God.[29] Visitations from the dead in Mormon temples are regarded as a positive experience by many Mormons.[30] Few Mormons realize that the "ancient" endowment ritual has undergone many significant changes since 1845, the most recent in 2005.

10 Q: Does Mormonism Teach Polygamy?

Mormonism Claims...

Once Essential

Between 1852 and 1890 the practice of polygamy became essential for any Mormon hoping to achieve exaltation. Brigham Young proclaimed that the "only men who become Gods, even the Sons of God, are those who enter into polygamy."[31]

Still Valid

Though it was necessary for Mormon leaders to formally renounce plural marriage in 1890, the principle remains valid, and the earthly practice of polygamy will one day resume. "Obviously the holy practice will commence again after the Second Coming of the Son of Man and the ushering in of the millennium."[32]

Portrait of sixth president Joseph F. Smith and family
Source: Utah State Historical Society

A: The Bible Teaches...

Never Encouraged

There is no denying that great men such as Abraham, Jacob, David, and Solomon practiced plural marriage. However, the practice of polygamy never had any bearing on an individual's personal salvation. Instead, we find polygamy being *tolerated* by God rather than commanded by him, because it often caused conflict and sometimes led the family into idolatry. Monogamy was always the rule, and polygamy was always the exception. A man was to cleave to his wife (not wives), and as Jesus confirmed, these "two" shall become one (Gen. 2:24; Mark 10:8). Paul wrote that every man should have his own wife and every woman her own husband (1 Cor. 7:2), assuming monogamy as the norm. This pattern is also expected for those seeking office in the church (1 Tim. 3:2; Titus 1:6). The New Testament never condones anything but a relationship between one man and one woman.

You Should Also Know...

Jacob 2:24 in the Book of Mormon condemns the plural marriages of David and Solomon; however, Jacob 2:30 states that God could allow polygamy should he wish to "raise up seed." Many Mormon apologists have argued that this nullifies any contradiction some see in verse 24. However, during the polygamy era in Utah there were more men than women, making polygamy unnecessary.[33] Furthermore, Jacob 2:30 certainly was not the basis for Joseph Smith's plural wives. Though the doctrine of polygamy was announced publicly in 1852, it was being practiced secretly by a select few leaders long before that date. Mormon historian Richard L. Bushman concedes, "All told, ten of Joseph's plural wives were married to other men."[34]

Tips for Talking with Mormons

Don't assume that a Mormon defines a word in the same way you do.

Do define your terms — and have them define theirs. (For example, "What do you believe about salvation? About eternal life? Are they the same, or different?")

Don't assume what an individual Mormon believes. Not all Mormons agree with their leaders. This could be because they are not aware of what their leaders have taught. For example, if a Mormon appears to answer a question biblically, you may respond by saying something like, "That is exactly what the Bible teaches; however, are you aware that prophet so-and-so said just the opposite? Shouldn't they be in harmony with the Bible if they are getting their information from the same God who gave us the Bible?"

Do ask Mormons what they believe. Rather than accusing, ask a question.

Don't dwell on topics that are especially sensitive to Mormons and should only be addressed after they feel more comfortable discussing religious issues with you. Talking about the temple ceremony, the sacred garments, polygamy, or racism will almost certainly bring the discussion to a close. Use your time wisely.

Do concentrate on core issues. What the Mormon believes about God the Father, Jesus Christ, and the Holy Spirit, as well as the issue of salvation, should be primary. Do your Mormon acquaintances have the assurance that when they die all of their sins are forgiven? Do they feel confident they will receive the best their religion has to offer (godhood, eternal increase)? If so, how so? If not, why not?

Don't be surprised if Mormons are suspicious of Christian literature. Mormons often feel that information written about their church, but not *by* their church, is almost always inaccurate. If you do use Christian material, make sure it is well-documented. Rather than insisting that the material is correct, have Mormons show you where the information could be wrong. To do this they will need to read the material and check the references.

Do memorize certain points and quotes. This often works better than using printed material because it shows the Mormon that you have taken the time to read LDS resources. Quote directly from LDS sources if possible. Statements from LDS leaders work best.

Don't think you need to cover every topic in one sitting. Sometimes dealing with one or two subjects makes it easier to remember what you talked about.

Do be patient. Mormons are led to believe that leaving the LDS church will lead to damnation. This is not a decision most Mormons make in an instant.

Quick Facts

Names: Church of Jesus Christ of Latter-day Saints (official); Mormon Church, LDS Church (informal)

Year/Place Founded: 1830 in Fayette, New York (USA), originally as the "Church of Christ"

Founder: Joseph Smith, Jr. (1805–1844)

World Headquarters: Salt Lake City, Utah (USA)

Estimated Adherents: Over 14 million in more than 160 nations and territories (2010)

Full-Time Missionaries: 52,000 including those on "special service" assignments

Materials Include: Include Book of Mormon (over 160 languages)

Temples: Over 130 in more than 40 countries

Terms and Definitions

Adam: According to Doctrine and Covenants (D&C) 27:11, Adam is Michael the Archangel, the Ancient of Days. He will one day return to the Garden of Eden (located in western Missouri, at a place called Adam-ondi-Ahman; D&C 116:1).

Apostasy: In general use, a falling away from one's faith. Mormonism teaches that Christianity became completely apostate after the death of the original apostles, making it necessary for God to restore it.

Baptism for the Dead: Temple ritual in which a Mormon "proxy" (living person) is baptized on behalf of a deceased person.

Book of Mormon: Translated by Joseph Smith from gold plates he allegedly received from the angel Moroni. The plates are believed to contain a record of ancient American inhabitants who are descendants of the "House of Israel." After being translated, the plates were taken back to heaven.

Celestial Kingdom: The highest kingdom of glory awaiting faithful Latter-day Saints. Entrance into this kingdom is gained by complete obedience to the Mormon gospel.

Endowment Ceremony: Secret temple ritual performed by living persons, sometimes on behalf of the dead. Required for exaltation.

Eternal Increase: The ability for exalted persons to procreate throughout eternity.

Eternal Life: Also known as individual salvation, exaltation, or godhood. Eternal life is only gained by faithful Mormons who keep all of the commandments (celestial law).

Exaltation: Synonymous with eternal life. Only those who gain exaltation have the ability to become gods and procreate throughout eternity.

First Vision: An event that Mormons claim took place in the spring of 1820 in which God the Father and Jesus Christ appeared to Joseph Smith and told him that all the churches were wrong, and that their creeds were an abomination.

God the Father: Also known as Heavenly Father or Elohim. The God of Mormonism was once a human and currently inhabits a body of flesh and bones.

Jesus Christ: The literally begotten son of God the Father and Heavenly Mother. The Jesus of Mormonism is the firstborn of God's offspring, including all angels, demons, and humans.

Joseph Smith: The founder of the Latter-day Saint movement. He is considered to be a modern-day prophet who was called by God to restore "true Christianity" to the earth after centuries of apostasy. He died in 1844 during a gun battle with an angry mob while incarcerated in Carthage, Illinois.

Mormon: A Nephite leader; father of Moroni. It is Mormon from whom the Book of Mormon gets its name. Also, a nickname given to followers of Joseph Smith and the church he founded.

Moroni: The son of Mormon. Moroni buried the gold plates containing the Book of Mormon and later appeared as an angel to Joseph Smith to tell him of their location. His image is found on many LDS temples throughout the world.

Nephites and Lamanites: According to the Book of Mormon, followers of Nephi and Laman, the sons of the Prophet Lehi who led his family to the New World prior to the capture of Jerusalem (around 600 BC). Those who followed the wicked Laman were shown God's displeasure by being cursed with a dark skin (2 Nephi 5:21–25); they are considered the ancestors of the American Indians and Polynesians.

Priesthood: The priesthood gives Mormon males the power and authority to act on behalf of God. It consists of two orders: the Aaronic Priesthood (the lesser priesthood) and the Melchizedek (the higher priesthood). Males of African descent were denied the Mormon priesthood until 1978.

Repentance: Involves confessing and forsaking sin (D&C 58:43). Only Mormons who abandon their sins are considered truly repentant.

Salvation by Grace: Also known as general salvation. All humans, by the fact that they are resurrected from the dead, are "saved by grace," though most never receive eternal life.

Standard Works: Includes the Bible, Book of Mormon, Doctrine and Covenants, and Pearl of Great Price. Only the Bible is accepted with qualification and is not to be fully trusted.

Temples: Special buildings reserved for ordinances for the dead, marriages for "time and eternity," and "sealings" of families for eternity.

Resources

The inclusion of a work does not necessarily mean endorsement of all its contents or of other works by the same author(s).

LITERATURE

Christian Authors/Publishers

Answering Mormons' Questions by Bill McKeever (Bethany House, 1991)

Inside Today's Mormonism by Richard Abanes (Harvest House, 2004)

By His Own Hand Upon Papyrus: A New Look at the Joseph Smith Papyri by Charles M. Larson (Institute for Religious Research, 1992)

Mormon America: The Power and the Promise by Richard and Joan Ostling (Harper One, rev. ed. 2007)

Mormonism 101 by Bill McKeever and Eric Johnson (Baker Books, 2000)

One Nation Under Gods by Richard Abanes (Thunder's Mouth Press, 2003)

Speaking the Truth in Love to Mormons by Mark Cares (WELS Outreach Resources, 1998)

The Rise of Mormonism by H. Michael Marquardt (Xulon Press, 2005)

What Every Mormon (and Non-Mormon) Should Know by Edmund Gruss and Lane Thuet (Xulon Press, 2006)

Mormon Authors/Publishers

An Insider's View of Mormon Origins by Grant Palmer (Signature Books, 2002)

Early Mormonism and the Magic World View by D. Michael Quinn (Signature Books, 1998)

In Sacred Loneliness: The Plural Wives of Joseph Smith by Todd Compton (Signature Books, 1997)

Mormon Polygamy: A History by Richard S. Van Wagoner (Signature Books, 1992 [2nd ed.])

VIDEO/DVD

Burying the Past: Legacy of the Mountain Meadows Massacre (Patrick Film Productions, 2003)

DNA vs. the Book of Mormon (Living Hope Ministries, 2005)

Mormonism's Greatest Problems (Truth in Depth, 2004)

Speaking the Truth in Love to Mormons (WELS Media, n.d.)

The Bible vs. the Book of Mormon (Living Hope Ministries, 2005)

The Lost Book of Abraham (Institute for Religious Research, 2002)

The Mormon Puzzle (North American Missions Board, 1997)

POWERPOINT®

10 Questions & Answers on Mormonism (Rose Publishing, Inc., 2006)

INTERNET

Christian Research and Counsel   www.crcmin.org
Concerned Christians   www.concernedchristians.org
Living Hope Ministries   www.lhvm.org
Mormonwiki   www.mormonwiki.org
Mormonism Research Ministry   www.mrm.org

Mormons in Transition   www.irr.org/mit
Truth in Love to Mormons   www.truthinlovetomormons.com
Utah Lighthouse Ministry   www.utlm.org

SOURCE REFERENCES

1   *The Great Apostasy*, Preface, p. iii
2   Joseph Smith — History 1:19
3   Doctrine and Covenants 135:3
4   *Teachings of the Prophet Joseph Smith*, p. 194
5   *Doctrines of Salvation*, Vol. 1, p. 188
6   Doctrine and Covenants 87
7   *Journal of Discourses*, Vol. 7, p. 289; *Gospel Truth*, Vol. 1, p. 255 [1974 ed]
8   *The Millennial Messiah*, p. 334
9   *Mormon Doctrine*, p. 169
10 First Presidency letter of May 22, 1992
11 *History of the Church*, Vol. 1, p. 368
12 8th Article of Faith
13 "Letter Reaffirms Use of King James Version of Bible," *Church News*, June 20, 1992, p. 3
14 *Divine Authenticity of the Book of Mormon*, p. 47
15 *Gospel Principles*, p. 53
16 *Teachings of the Prophet Joseph Smith*, p. 345
17 *The Teachings of Lorenzo Snow*, p. 1
18 *Doctrine and Covenants* 130:22
19 *Journal of Discourses*, Vol. 2, p. 345
20 *Gospel Principles*, p. 64
21 Book of Mormon, 3 Nephi
22 *Ensign*, May 1988, p. 53
23 Mormon apostle John A. Widtsoe, *Joseph Smith — Seeker after Truth, Prophet of God*, p. 170
24 Moroni 10:32
25 Spencer W. Kimball, *The Miracle of Forgiveness*, p. 212
26 *Gospel Principles*, p. 253
27 *The Miracle of Forgiveness*, pp. 208–209
28 *Teachings of the Prophet Joseph Smith*, pp. 193, 356
29 *Discourses of Brigham Young*, p. 416
30 As fourth LDS president Wilford Woodruff observed, "The dead will be after you, they will seek after you as they have after us in [the temple at] St. George [Utah]" (*Journal of Discourses*, Vol. 19, p. 229).
31 *Journal of Discourses*, Vol. 11, p. 269
32 Bruce R. McConkie, *Mormon Doctrine*, 2d ed., p. 578
33 "The United States census records from 1850 to 1940, and all available Church records, uniformly show a preponderance of males in Utah, and in the Church" (apostle John Widtsoe, *Evidences and Reconciliations*, p. 391).
34 *Joseph Smith: Rough Stone Rolling*, p. 439

General Editor: Paul Carden, Executive Director, Centers for Apologetics Research (CFAR). Principal Author: Bill McKeever, Founder and Director, Mormonism Research Ministry. Contributor: Robert M. Bowman, Jr., MA in Biblical Studies & Theology.

10 Keys to Witnessing to Cults

Share the Truth with Respect

- Strategic Questions
- Responses to Common Objections
- Help in Identifying Cultic Doctrine
- Tips for Talking with Ex-Cultists

WHAT IS A CULT?

As cult expert Alan Gomes has stated, "cults grow out of and deviate from a previously established religion."

Therefore, a cult of Christianity would be a group of people who claim to be Christian yet hold to "a particular doctrinal system" set forth by a leader, group of leaders, or organization which "denies … one or more of the central doctrines of the Christian faith." (Ron Rhodes, *The Challenge of the Cults and New Religions*; Grand Rapids, MI: Zondervan, 2001)

Christianity's central doctrines include:

- God (Trinity)
- The deity and work of Jesus Christ on the cross
- Humanity's sinfulness
- Salvation by grace alone through faith
- The authority of Scripture

Cults of Christianity are groups whose claims about these central doctrines contradict what the Bible teaches including …

> **Jehovah's Witnesses**
> **Mormonism**
> **Christian Science**
> **The Family/Children of God**
> **Unification Church**
> **Christadelphians**
> **Oneness Pentecostalism**

but excluding other groups such as …

> **Scientology** (no direct relation to a previously established religion, despite the cross in their logo)
> **Hare Krishna** (no biblical basis claimed; little reference to Jesus)

Three main types of injury from false beliefs:

Physical—In some cases, followers of Christian Science have died because they rejected medical treatment, believing that sickness and death are illusions. Jehovah's Witnesses have lost their lives because they refused blood transfusions, believing the cult's teaching that receiving a blood transfusion violates Jehovah's law. In these and other groups, people have unwittingly believed something and lost.

Emotional—Members of a cult often feel extreme guilt because they're trapped in a system in which they have to earn their salvation—the standards being so high that they can never completely measure up. They are required to obey the cult's rules precisely, and if they fail, they're not saved.

Spiritual—Cults proclaim a different Jesus by denying what the Bible teaches about who Jesus is and what he did for us on the cross. Thus, they redefine the gospel of salvation. If people have a counterfeit Jesus with a counterfeit gospel, then they have a counterfeit salvation.

To witness effectively, you need a strategy. Following these key points will greatly increase your success when cultists show up on your doorstep.

1 KNOW BASIC BIBLE TEACHINGS

No one can know all the false teachings of all the cults, but Christians can learn the Bible well enough so that they will recognize cultic doctrine.

Bankers are trained to recognize counterfeit currency by studying genuine dollar bills. Thus, bankers will recognize a counterfeit bill when they come across it. The more a person understands the Bible, the better that person will be able to recognize cultic errors.

Scripture warns about spiritual deception. Galatians 1:8 speaks of "a gospel other than the one we preached to you." Second Corinthians 11:4 warns us to avoid those who preach "[another] Jesus ... a different spirit ... a different gospel."

Cults often deny or distort three key biblical doctrines:

- The **Trinity**—one God in three Persons
- The person and work of **Jesus Christ**
- The gospel of **salvation** by grace alone through faith

Memorize key apologetic verses and central doctrines:

If a Jehovah's Witness says that the Holy Spirit is a force and not a person, show him or her passages that demonstrate that the Holy Spirit is a person: 1 Corinthians 2:11–12; 12:11; Ephesians 4:30; Romans 8:26-27.

The Trinity:

- **There is only one God**— Isaiah 43:10-11; 44:6,8; 45:21-22; 46:9; John 17:3; 1 John 5:20-21.

- **Father is God**—1 Peter 1:2; Philippians 2:11

- **Son is God**—Matthew 1:23; John 1:1; 20:28; Hebrews 1:8; 2 Peter 1:1; Titus 2:13

- **Holy Spirit is God**—Acts 5:3-4; 1 Corinthians 3:16-17; 2 Corinthians 3:17

The Person of Jesus Christ:

- **He is eternal and uncreated**— Isaiah 9:6; Hebrews 7:3; Micah 5:2; John 1:1-3; 8:58; Colossians 1:15-19

- **He retained his deity while becoming a man**—Philippians 2:5-11; Colossians 1:19; 2:9; Hebrews 1:3-8

- **He is equal in nature to God the Father**—John 5:18; John 19:7

- **He receives the same honor and worship as the Father**—John 5:23; Hebrews 1:6; Revelation 5:11-14; John 14:14

The Gospel of Salvation:

- **Salvation is a free gift**— Romans 6:23; 1 John 5:11-13

- **Salvation is by faith alone apart from works**—Acts 16:30-31; John 5:24; 6:28-29,47; Ephesians 2:8-9; Titus 3:5; Romans 3:28; 4:4-8; 8:1; 11:6; Galatians 3:1-3; Philippians 3:9

- **Works are the natural result of saving faith**—Eph. 2:10; James 2:14

2 DON'T ASSUME EVERY CULTIST BELIEVES THE SAME THING

For example, individual Mormons often have different levels of knowledge:

- Some Mormons follow the rules so well that they're given a "recommend"—a pass that lets them enter the Mormon temple and learn secret things that less "worthy" members don't learn.

- Some Mormons are more knowledgeable because they pay attention to the messages given by the church's "living prophet," or study well before their two-year missionary service to represent the church, while others don't prepare as much.

So, don't tell a person what he or she believes. Instead, ask questions that end up in a constructive discussion that leads to an examination of biblical doctrine.

QUESTIONS TO OPEN A DISCUSSION:
GOD:

- Who do you believe God is?
- Do you believe there is only one true God?
- Do you believe in the Trinity: God in three persons: Father, Son, Holy Spirit?
- Do you believe God has always existed?

JESUS CHRIST:

- Who do you believe Jesus Christ is?
- Do you believe Jesus has always existed, or was he created?
- Do you believe Jesus is God? Is he equal to the Father in his divine nature?
- Do you believe Jesus earned his Godhood or has he always been God?
- Do you believe Jesus physically and bodily rose from the dead?

THE GOSPEL OF SALVATION:

- What do you believe a person has to do to be saved?
- Do you believe a person has to join your religion to be saved?
- Do you believe a person will lose salvation if that person leaves your religion?
- At what point do you know that you've done enough to be assured of eternal life?

3 CULTISTS ARE TRAINED TO ANSWER OBJECTIONS

Many who have talked with Jehovah's Witnesses and Mormons would say that they seem to have an answer for everything.

The reason they seem to have answers for every question is because they've been carefully trained, and often have months—or years—of practice. For example, active Jehovah's Witnesses not only go door-to-door responding to householders' objections, but they have weekly training sessions where they learn what to say to someone like you.

So, what is the solution? Simply move the discussion back to the Bible. Don't worry if they are giving you rote responses that they have memorized. Just keep presenting evidence that their leaders are not telling them the truth and keep taking them back to the Bible. Eventually, the rote responses will stop.

One helpful technique is to request that they read a particular verse aloud, and then ask: "What is being said here?" If they repeat the typical cultic interpretation, ask them to read it aloud again, slowly and carefully—and follow it with another question. If you are persistent, you'll help them see for themselves the contradictions and problems with their view.

Note also that cultists are trained how to respond to common comebacks. For example, they are taught how to respond if people say: "I'm not interested," "I have my own religion," "We are already Christians here," "I'm busy," "Why do you people call so often?," "I am already well acquainted with your work," or "We have no money." When someone raises such an objection, this automatically triggers a response in the mind of the cultist. Keeping this fact in mind will help you to remain patient with the cultist.

4 CHECK SCRIPTURES

When cultists quote a verse it is typically out of context.

Never take the cultist's interpretation of a passage at face value because they often misinterpret the passage to suit their own agenda.

For example, the Bahá'ís claim that their prophet Bahá'u'lláh was prophesied by Jesus in John 14:16. In that passage, Jesus talked about "another Counselor," and the Bahá'í cult says that Jesus was referring to Bahá'u'lláh who would come in the nineteenth century. But the Bahá'ís completely distort the teachings of Jesus, because Jesus identifies the Counselor as the Holy Spirit in verse 26. Jesus said that the Holy Spirit would come in a few days (Acts 1:5), not in the nineteenth century. Jesus said that the Holy Spirit would be with us forever, but Bahá'u'lláh died after a few decades. Also, Jesus

said that the Holy Spirit would remind us of everything he had taught, not that he would teach entirely different doctrines from an entirely different prophet. Going to the verse and looking it up in context dispels the mythological interpretation imposed upon it by the cult.

Another example is the Jehovah's Witnesses' claim that the Bible condemns birthdays in Matthew 14:6-10, because it says that on Herod's birthday, he had John the Baptist executed. However, this passage proves only that Herod was evil, not that birthdays are evil. One will search this passage and other passages in vain to find a single statement where God explicitly condemns birthday celebrations.

Remember these things when interpreting Scripture:

Always examine the context of the verse quoted by cultists. Ask: Who is speaking in this passage? What is the setting? Who is being addressed? What is the main point of the passage? Look to the context for answers to these questions.

Interpreting Scripture is about drawing the meaning out of the Bible verses, not putting a meaning onto the verses. Ask the cultist: Where does this passage clearly teach what you are claiming?

If a verse is unclear, examine it in light of clear passages. Bible verses are not disconnected fragments, but are embedded in the whole of Scripture. Ask: What does the Bible clearly teach in other places? How does the overall teaching in the Bible on this subject help us understand what this particular verse means?

5 DEFINE TERMS

There is a communication block between the cultist and the Christian that can be removed by defining key Christian words and ideas.

Consider, for example, this phrase: "Jesus Christ is the Son of God. He died for the sins of mankind, and then resurrected from the dead. Scripture speaks of his second coming." Jehovah's Witnesses, Mormons, and many other cults would all agree with this statement, but they would interpret it differently from the traditional Christian view.

Jehovah's Witnesses will say:

- "Yes, Jesus is the Christ"—but they would argue that Jesus was not the "Christ" at his birth, but became the "Christ" at his baptism.

- "Yes, Jesus is the Son of God"—but they view the term "Son of God" as a lesser "god" than God the Father because they claim Jesus was created by God.

- "Yes, Jesus died for the sins of mankind"—but they would say that his blood covers one's sin only if one proves oneself worthy through door-to-door activity.

- "Yes, Jesus was resurrected"—but they will say it was not a physical resurrection. Instead, he was resurrected spiritually as Michael the Archangel.

- "Yes, Scripture speaks of his second coming"— but they claim that this prophecy is already in the process of being fulfilled through an "invisible presence" of Christ in 1914.

Mormons will say:

- "Yes, Jesus is the Christ"—but they would add that Jesus had to compete with Lucifer over who would be the savior of the world.

- "Yes, Jesus is the Son of God"—but they would say that he is the "Son" only because he was born in heaven as a spirit baby to God the Father and one of his spirit wives.

- "Yes, Jesus died for the sins of mankind"—but they would claim that the majority of his atonement took place in the Garden of Gethsemane, rather than on the cross.

- "Yes, Jesus' blood covers the sins of mankind"—but they would add works as a requirement for entrance into the highest level of heaven.

Mormons, Jehovah's Witnesses, and other cults *mean something entirely different by their use of these traditional Christian terms. Never assume you are communicating clearly in a conversation unless you have taken the time to define your terms biblically.*

6 ASK STRATEGIC QUESTIONS

You can't force good doctrine on a person trapped in a cult; instead, ask questions that cause him or her to think critically.

Examples of Strategic Questions for Mormons:

▶ If you're talking with a Mormon who thinks that human beings can become gods, ask: How do you interpret Isaiah 43:10, which reads, "Before me no god was formed, nor will there be one after me"?

▶ If the Bible has many mistakes, as Mormons claim, why does the Mormon church continue to publish and distribute the King James Version to church members?

▶ I noticed Mormon churches do not display the cross. Since Paul gloried " in the cross" of Christ (Galatians 6:14), why don't Mormons glory in it as well? Do you believe the atonement took place on the cross or in the garden of Gethsemane? If the Mormon answers that most of the atonement took place in the garden, ask: Why did Jesus have to die on the cross if his suffering in the garden atoned for the majority of our sins?

▶ If the Mormon asks you to pray about the Book of Mormon, ask: Which Book of Mormon do you want me to pray about? The 1830 edition? The 1921 edition? Or today's edition, which has over 4,000 changes from the original 1830 edition?

Examples of Strategic Questions for Jehovah's Witnesses:

▶ If the Jehovah's Witnesses are the only true witnesses for God, and if the Jehovah's Witnesses as an organization came into being in the late nineteenth century (which is a historical fact), does this mean God was without a witness for over eighteen centuries throughout church history?

▶ If Jesus is Michael the Archangel, why was Jesus able to rebuke Satan at Matthew 16:23 when Michael didn't have the authority to rebuke Satan at Jude 9?

▶ According to Acts 1:8, 2:32, 3:15, 4:33, and 13:30-31, were the early Christians witnesses of Jehovah or witnesses of Jesus Christ?

▶ If there is no other Savior than God (Isaiah 43:11), then doesn't this mean that New Testament references to Jesus as Savior point to his deity (Titus 2:13)?

7 BE LOVING

It's not just what you say, it's how you say it!

Sharing your faith isn't just about strong answers from the Bible; it's about being sold out to Jesus Christ. If a person knows all the right answers but is arrogant, prideful, and has an "in your face" attitude, this isn't the kind of person who is going to draw people to the real Jesus.

So, unless the situation calls for it, try to avoid a highly confrontational approach. For example, you could say to a Mormon: "My friend, you worship a false god proclaimed by a false prophet and a false book called the Book of Mormon and a false gospel based upon works." And you'd be technically correct! But that approach may turn the Mormon off to the true message you are trying to communicate. You may win the argument, but lose the Mormon.

Consider a gentler approach in which you say, "My friend, I really care about you, and I'm afraid you might get deceived into believing a lie. I'm afraid you might die and go into eternity believing something that isn't true. Can we talk about this? Can I share with you why I believe the Bible is true?" Focus on keeping a loving attitude in your heart.

Let your love be genuine and embracing. People can sense if you truly care about them, as opposed to merely acting like you care only because you want to convert them. Pray that the Holy Spirit would fill your heart with love that shows itself in meaningful ways to your cultic acquaintances. This kind of love is sacrificial and self-giving, and involves showing hospitality to people (Ephesians 5:2; 1 Timothy 4:12; 1 Corinthians 16:14).

You'll be amazed at what God will do through a person who is sold out to Jesus Christ, allowing Jesus' grace and love to flow through him or her when approaching someone in a cult. Strong answers from that kind of person mean a lot. Let Jesus' love shine through you!

If the cultist becomes a Christian, the love has to continue. There's a good chance that his cult will expel him, and nearly everyone in his life will shun him. He may also lose his family, so he will need to be brought into a new family. As his new brothers and sisters in Christ, you must make sure that he feels at home in his new church and that discipleship is an ongoing priority. Part of being loving means that you don't drop the ball at conversion but help him to become a true, lifelong disciple of Christ.

8 DEMONSTRATE JESUS' DEITY

Cultists always get the identity of Jesus wrong.

To witness effectively to cultists, you will need to be prepared to show the cultist that Jesus is the eternal God. Here's one way to do this: Compare the Old Testament descriptions and attributes of God with the New Testament descriptions and attributes of Jesus Christ.

Descriptions and Attributes	God in the Old Testament	Jesus in the New Testament
Creator	Isaiah 44:24	Colossians 1:16; John 1:3
Savior	Isaiah 43:11	Titus 2:13–14; Jude 4
Shepherd	Psalm 23:1-2	John 10:11-18
Great Judge	Psalm 98:9	John 5:21-22
First and Last	Isaiah 44:6; 48:12	Revelation 1:17-18
Holy One	Isaiah 47:4	Acts 3:14; John 6:69
Glory	Isaiah 6:1–5	John 12:41
Omnipotent (all-powerful)	Jeremiah 32:17, 27	Matthew 19:26
Omniscient (all-knowing)	Psalm 147:5	1 John 3:20
Omnipresent (present everywhere)	Jeremiah 23:24	Matthew 28:20
Gives Eternal Life	Deuteronomy 30:20	Romans 6:23

With these verses, the cultist will likely go home with a different view of Jesus. If that happens, God the Holy Spirit will be working on his or her heart, convicting and bringing to mind the things of Jesus Christ.

CHRISTIAN RESPONSES TO OBJECTIONS COMMONLY RAISED BY CULTISTS

The word "Trinity" is not found in the Bible and is therefore not a biblical idea. Just because a word is not found in the Bible, doesn't mean that it is not a biblical concept. For example, the word "theocracy" (God-ruled nation) is not in the Bible, yet Israel was a theocracy. In the same way, the Trinity concept is seen throughout Scripture.

The Trinity is confusing, so God would not exist as a Trinity. Finite humans cannot fully comprehend God, who is infinite (Isaiah 55:8).

Jesus is God's Son and is "with" God, so cannot be God himself. Jesus is the second person of the Trinity, distinct from —and yet equal in nature to—the Father (Jn. 1:1; Col. 2:9). As God's "Son," he possesses God's full nature (Jn. 5:18; 19:7; Lev. 24:16).

Jesus said the Father is greater than him, so he cannot be "equal" to God (John14:28). In his human nature, the Father was "greater" than Jesus, but in his God nature, Jesus is equal to the Father (Jn. 5:18).

Since God is invisible and cannot die, Jesus cannot be God. Jesus' is the visible "image" of the invisible God (Jn. 1:18; 14:9; Heb. 1:3; 2 Cor. 4:4). He died in his humanity, but in his deity, he remained alive (Phil. 2:5-11; Jn. 2:18-22).

9 EMPHASIZE THE GOSPEL

Cultists need to hear about God's grace more than anything else!

You can ask any cultist, "At what point in your religion do you know for sure that when you die you will be saved and accepted by God?" The cultist will not be able to give a definite answer, because his or her salvation is dependant upon performance.

For example, Mormons are told that they must prove themselves worthy to be accepted by God into the highest level of heaven. While many Mormons believe that they have all eternity to work toward perfection, most will readily admit that they are not far along in the process of achieving it. Also, many believe the statement in Mormon scripture that says, "Go your ways and sin no more; but unto that soul who sinneth shall the former sins return, saith the Lord your God" (Doctrine and Covenants 82:7). This is why a Mormon Church manual explains that, "Those who receive forgiveness and then repeat the sin are held accountable for their former sins" (*Gospel Principles*, 1978, 1992 ed., p. 253).

Mormons are under a heavy burden to constantly strive to confess and forsake their sins. Never can a Mormon say that he has full assurance that he is forgiven, because at any moment, he may repeat a sin that will make him "accountable" for his former sins.

This weight on the cultists' shoulders is unbearable. No one can survive this kind of legalism. How much better is the wonderful grace of God!

"For it is by grace you have been saved, through faith— and this not from yourselves, it is the gift of God—not by works, so that no one can boast." —Ephesians 2:8–9

"Though your sins are like scarlet, they shall be as white as snow; though they are red as crimson, they shall be like wool." —Isaiah 1:18

"In [Jesus] we have redemption through his blood, the forgiveness of sins, in accordance with the riches of God's grace." —Ephesians 1:7

"Their sins and lawless acts I will remember no more." —Hebrews 10:17

"Blessed is he whose transgressions are forgiven, whose sins are covered." —Psalm 32:1

10 GIVE YOUR TESTIMONY

Cultists need to hear what God has done in your life.

You might not be an expert in theology, the Bible, cultic doctrines, or apologetics, but you are an expert in what Jesus has done in your life! You are an expert in how Jesus has set you free. When you give your testimony, focus on the mighty river of God's grace. When a cultist sees that you know you're a sinner who deserves to spend eternity apart from God, but you have absolute assurance that you are saved because of what Jesus has done for you, that will make an impact on the cultist.

KEEP THE FOLLOWING THINGS IN MIND WHEN GIVING YOUR TESTIMONY:

▶ **Describe what your life was like** before you were a Christian. What were your feelings, attitudes, actions, and relationships like during this time? (The apostle Paul clearly spoke of what his life was like before he was a Christian—Acts 26:4-11.)

▶ **What events transpired** in your life that led up to your decision to trust in Christ? What caused you to begin considering Christ as a solution to your needs? Be specific.

▶ **Describe your conversion experience.** Was it a book you read? Were you in a church? Were other Christians with you at the time? (Paul clearly spoke of how he became a Christian—Acts 26:12-18.)

▶ **What kind of change took place** in your life following your conversion? What effect did trusting in Christ have on your feelings, attitudes, actions, and relationships? (Paul spoke of how his life changed once becoming a Christian —Acts 26:19-23.)

▶ **Never forget that God works through people.** He uses people as instruments to reach out and bless other people; that's his chosen means. In the Old Testament God worked through Israel to bring blessing to others. The Jewish nation would be a light to the Gentiles, an instrument by which blessing would be communicated to all people everywhere. In the New Testament, the church is to be used as an instrument of God by which God reaches through his church to bring blessing to people around the world. Each one of us can be used as an instrument!

TALKING WITH EX-CULTISTS

DO let the ex-cultist know he or she is not alone. Help the person find a Christian support group of ex-members (many are on the Internet at www.meetup.com), and give the person ex-member testimonies to read. (For example, see the testimonies at www.4mormon.org and www.4jehovah.org.)

DO NOT pressure the ex-cultist into church attendance or Christian activities too soon. Remember that in the cult, meeting attendance was likely mandatory; so a simple, "I missed you at church last night; where were you?" question from a well-meaning Christian can scare off an ex-cultist.

DO demonstrate the love of Christ by unconditionally accepting the ex-cultist regardless of his or her issues with Christianity. Remember that in the cult, it was not acceptable to act or believe differently, so be sensitive to the ex-cultist's insecurity about the commitment level of your friendship.

DO create a "safe" environment for the ex-cultist to ask his or her questions. Never belittle the person's ideas or questions or put them down by saying, "I would never believe …" or "I would never do …"

DO help the ex-cultist feel accepted and normal. Remember that ex-cultists already feel inferior because of their prior involvement in a cult, and most would not have joined the cult if they had known all the facts.

DO NOT tell the ex-cultist WHAT to think, but HOW to think. Remember that in the cult, members were not allowed to think for themselves; so the ex-cultist will need to learn how to research and find answers to the questions they have about God, the Bible, and Christianity.

DO point the ex-cultist to a relationship with Jesus. Ex-cultists are hungry for something to believe in and belong to. As a result, people often leave one cult only to join another. Instead of pointing them to your church or another religious association, you must point them to Jesus. Emphasize that he is the only one who can fulfill the deepest longings of the human heart.

RESOURCES

The inclusion of a work or web site does not necessarily mean the endorsement of all its contents or of other works by the same author(s) or organization.

LITERATURE

General

The Challenge of the Cults and New Religions by Ron Rhodes (Zondervan, 2001)

Correcting the Cults: Expert Responses to Their Scripture Twisting by Norman L. Geisler and Ron Rhodes (Baker, 2005)

Scripture Twisting: Twenty Ways the Cults Misread the Bible by James Sire (InterVarsity, 1980)

A Guide to New Religious Movements by Ronald Enroth, ed. (InterVarsity, 2005)

Cults and the Occult, 4th ed. by Edmond C. Gruss (P&R, 2002)

Charts of Cults, Sects & Religious Movements by H. Wayne House (Zondervan, 2000)

So What's the Difference?: A Look at 20 Worldviews, Faiths and How They Compare to Christianity by Fritz Ridenour (Gospel Light, 2001)

The Unexpected Journey: Conversations with People Who Turned from Other Beliefs to Jesus by Thom S. Rainer (Zondervan, 2005)

Cults in Our Midst by Margaret Thaler Singer with Janja Lalich (Jossey-Bass, 2003)

Recovery from Cults: Help for Victims of Psychological and Spiritual Abuse by Michael Langone, ed. (W.W. Norton, 1993)

Mormonism

Reasoning from the Scriptures with the Mormons by Ron Rhodes and Marian Bodine (Harvest House, 1995)

Speaking the Truth in Love to Mormons by Mark Cares (WELS, 1998)

Where Does It Say That? by Bob Witte (WELS, 1998) www.irr.org/resources.html

Mormonism 101: Examining the Religion of the Latter-day Saints by Bill McKeever and Eric Johnson (Baker, 2000)

Jehovah's Witnesses

Reasoning from the Scriptures with the Jehovah's Witnesses by Ron Rhodes (Harvest House, 1993)

Jehovah's Witnesses Answered Verse by Verse by David A. Reed (Baker, 1986)

Jehovah's Witnesses by Robert M. Bowman, Jr. (Zondervan, 1995)

Other Groups

Mind Sciences by Todd Ehrenborg (Zondervan, 1995)

"Jesus Only" Churches by E. Calvin Beisner (Zondervan, 1995)

New Age Movement by Ron Rhodes (Zondervan, 1995)

POWERPOINT®

Christianity, Cults and Religions (Rose Publishing, 2010)

10 Questions and Answers on Mormonism (Rose Publishing, 2007)

10 Questions and Answers on Jehovah's Witnesses (Rose Publishing, 2007)

10 Keys to Witnessing to Cults (Rose Publishing, 2008)

Denominations Comparison (Rose Publishing, 2005)

Why Trust the Bible? (Rose Publishing, 2007)

INTERNET

Reasoning from the Scriptures Ministries www.RonRhodes.org

Witnesses for Jesus, Inc.   www.4witness.org

Watchman Fellowship   www.watchman.org

Personal Freedom Outreach   www.pfo.org

Evidence Ministries   www.evidenceministries.org

Mormons in Transition   www.irr.org/mit

Mormonism Research Ministry   www.mrm.org

TowerWatch Ministries   www.towerwatch.com

VIDEO/DVD

The Witness at Your Door and *The Witness Goes Out!* (Jeremiah Films, 1992)

In the Name of Jehovah (North American Mission Board, 2004)

Speaking the Truth in Love to Mormons (WELS media, n.d.) www.truthinloveministry.net/material.htm

The Mormon Puzzle (North American Mission Board, 1997)

The Bible vs. the Book of Mormon (Living Hope Ministries, 2005)

Principal Author: Ron Rhodes, ThD, President, Reasoning from the Scriptures Ministries
Co-Author: Christy (Harvey) Darlington, President, Witnesses for Jesus, Inc.

ROSE BIBLE BASICS:

Christianity, Cults & Religions

A FREE downloadable version of this study guide is available at
rose-publishing.com. Click on "News & Info," then on "Downloads."

The **leader guide** covers each chapter of this book and includes teaching tips,
additional resources, and answer keys for the study guide worksheets.
The **study guide** includes a reproducible worksheet and/or discussion
questions for each chapter.

What participants will gain from this study:
- Learn key facts, dates, writings, and basic beliefs of 30 cults and
religions.
- Be able to identify the differences and similarities between Christianity
and other religions.
- Learn the biblical warnings about the occult.
- Compare what the Bible teaches side by side with what Mormonism and
Jehovah's Witnesses teach.
- Understand the basics of Islam—and how to share your faith with
Muslims.
- Know how to effectively use the Bible when witnessing to people of
other faiths.

LEADER GUIDE

Spend time in prayer before each study session and pray for each participant.

CHAPTER 1: CHRISTIANITY, CULTS & RELIGIONS

Main Idea

Christians should study other religions to be able to recognize false and deceptive teachings, and to build bridges to help non-believers understand the gospel.

Teaching Tips

Introduce participants to the purposes of this study. Ask them what they hope to gain from the study or why they joined this study.

Because this chapter has so many groups it may be helpful to highlight the following:

- Jehovah's Witnesses, Mormonism, Unification Church, and Christian Science all use the Bible, but they believe different things about the Bible (e.g., not reliable or only reliable in their "translation;" not fully God's Word; other writings are superior). None of these groups believe in the Trinity.
- Salvation in Christianity is different than in Jehovah's Witnesses and Mormonism (for example, grace vs. works).
- The relationship of Judaism with Christianity has similarities and differences (for example, both use the Old Testament; believe in one personal God; practice prayer and repentance).
- Hinduism, Hare Krishna, TM, Buddhism and Soka Gakkai are eastern religions. Notice their similar beliefs about reincarnation, meditation, and who they say Jesus was.

Digging Deeper

During the discussion time, detailed questions about religions may arise. It may be helpful to have a world religions encyclopedia handy, such as *Nelson's Illustrated Guide to Religions* by James A. Beverley (Thomas Nelson, 2009).

Worksheet Key

(1) False (2) True (3) e (4) b (5) c

CHAPTER 2: CHRISTIANITY, CULTS & THE OCCULT

Main Idea

Occult practices are <u>not</u> innocent or harmless. God warns against and
condemns occult practices in the Bible.

Teaching Tips

Explain to participants the purposes of studying the occult: This study is not intended to
arouse and unhealthy curiosity about hidden and forbidden things. Instead, it is meant
to help discern danger so you can avoid it, resist it, and help others who are in it.

Before discussing the particular groups, cover the *Terms and Definitions* to
familiarize participants with the terms used (especially *occult, divination,
reincarnation, syncretism,* and *sorcery*).

Point out how Christian practices differ from occult practices:

- Magick is an attempt to manipulate reality according to what one wants.
  Following Jesus involves submitting our will to God's will, and miracles are
  God's doing, not ours.
- Divination is putting one's trust in inanimate objects. Seeking God's will is
  trusting in the Creator of all things.
- Channeling is opening oneself to evil spirits through secret methods and
  powers. Prayer is communicating with a loving God, and anyone (not just
  people with "special powers") can speak to God in prayer.

Digging Deeper

For more information on specific groups and what Christians are doing to reach
people involved in these groups, visit the Centers for Apologetics Research
(C/FAR) www.thecenters.org.

Worksheet Key

(1) a   (2) d   (3) a   (4) c   (5) c

CHAPTER 3: CHRISTIANITY & EASTERN RELIGIONS

Main Idea
Eastern religions are becoming increasingly influential. It is important for Christians to recognize which beliefs of eastern religions are <u>not</u> compatible with Christianity.

Teaching Tips
Because this chapter contains so much information, it may be helpful to focus the teaching time on the three common concepts of eastern religions—pantheism, reincarnation, and yoga/meditation—and on the *Key Beliefs* sections to compare each religion's core teachings with Christianity.

Questions may arise in the discussion time about whether it is OK for Christians to be involved in activities such as yoga, martial arts, acupuncture, and feng shui. When discussing this, consider these questions:
- Does the Bible specifically address this issue?
- What is the purpose of the activity?
- What methods are used in the activity?
- Is the activity affecting one's relationship with God?
- Is participation in the activity harming or helping one's Christian witness?

Digging Deeper
See the resources listed at the end of the chapter.

Worksheet Key
(1) b   (2) c   (3) b   (4) a   (5) d

CHAPTER 4: ISLAM & CHRISTIANITY

Main Idea

To effectively communicate with Muslims, Christians need to be aware of common misconceptions Muslims may hold about Christianity, as well as one's own misconceptions about Islam.

Teaching Tips

To open the discussion, ask participants to identify some examples in movies, TV shows, books, and magazines that depict Muslims. (Participants may not readily be able to think of examples, so in advance have a few examples of your own ready.) Ask: How were Muslims portrayed? If Christians were also depicted, how were they portrayed?

Have participants brainstorm things that Islam and Christianity have in common. Then list some the differences. Compare the lists side by side.

Digging Deeper

For a deeper understanding of Islam, see *Unveiling Islam* by Ergun Mehmet Caner and Emir Fethi Caner (Kregel, 2002).

Worksheet Key

(1) False   (2) True   (3) c   (4) c   (5) d

CHAPTERS 5: 10 Q&A ON JEHOVAH'S WITNESSES

Main Idea

Although Jehovah's Witnesses speak of Jesus, the Holy Spirit, salvation, and the Bible, their teachings are very different than what the Bible teaches.

Teaching Tips

Because covering all 10 Q&A may be too lengthy, compare instead how a Jehovah's Witness and a Christian might answer these questions:

1. Who is God?
2. Who is Jesus?
3. Who or what is the Holy Spirit?
4. Is the Bible reliable?
5. Where (or to whom) should people look for truth?
6. What does it mean to be "saved"?
7. How is someone saved?

Digging Deeper

See the resources listed at the end of the chapter.

Worksheet Key

(1) c   (2) True   (3) d   (4) b   (5) False

CHAPTER 6: 10 Q&A ON MORMONISM

Main Idea
Although many Mormons consider themselves to be Christian, Mormon beliefs are considerably different than what the Bible teaches.

Teaching Tips
Because covering all 10 Q&A may be too lengthy, compare instead how a Mormon and a Christian might answer these questions:

1. Who is God?
2. Who is Jesus?
3. What is the "Church"?
4. Where (or to whom) should people look for truth?
5. What does it mean to be "saved"?
6. How is someone saved?

Be sure to keep the conversation about Mormons respectful. You many need to remind participants that if we want to be able to be considerate when witnessing to Mormons (1 Peter 3:15), we need to avoid mocking them when talking about Mormonism when they're not present. Always remember to lead by example.

Digging Deeper
See the resources listed at the end of the chapter.

Worksheet Key
(1) a   (2) False   (3) False   (4) d   (5) False

CHAPTER 7: 10 KEYS TO WITNESSING TO CULTS

Main Idea

Cults leave people without the true gospel message. We can learn ways of effectively communicating the truth of Jesus Christ to people in cults.

Teaching Tips

Because this chapter uses many Jehovah's Witnesses and Mormon examples, it may be helpful to briefly review with participants the material covered in the previous two chapters.

This chapter focuses mostly on cults of Christianity, but some keys (such as 7 and 10) can be applied when witnessing to someone of any religion. However other keys (such as 8 and 3) may not be as helpful when talking with a person of another religion (like an eastern religion).

Practice Key #10: Give your testimony. Choose an option that would be fitting for your group: (1) Break participants into groups of four and let people share their testimony in these small groups; (2) Lead by example and give your own testimony during the session—or in advance ask one of the participants if he or she would be willing to give his or her testimony to the group; (3) Ask participants to write down their answers to the five bullet points under Key #10 and have an open sharing time with all participants. Be sure to make it clear to the group that if someone does not want to share their testimony that is OK—they can pass. Don't make it mandatory.

Digging Deeper

See the resources listed at the end of the chapter.

Worksheet Key

(1) c   (2) e   (3) False (cults *always* get the identity of Jesus wrong)   (4) d   (5) False

FEEDBACK

To improve future studies, be sure to get feedback from the group about teaching style, meeting location, discussion time, material covered, length of study, and group size. Choose a method that best suits your group: Anonymous evaluation sheet, e-mail response or questionnaire, open discussion. (See the feedback questions at the end of the study guide.)

Note: The inclusion of a work or website does not necessarily mean endorsement of all its contents or of other works by the same author(s).

STUDY GUIDE

The study guide which begins on the following page includes a reproducible worksheet and/or discussion questions for group discussion or personal reflection.

CHRISTIANITY, CULTS & RELIGIONS

Worksheet

1. True or False? Biblical Christianity teaches that those who will live with Jesus in heaven are saved by their individual good works.

2. True or False? Mormonism teaches that those who will be exalted to godhood are saved by their Mormon membership and works, such as baptism and tithing.

3. Christian Science teaches that Jesus:
   a. Displayed the "Christ" idea.
   b. Did not die on the cross.
   c. Is not literally coming again.
   d. (a) and (b)
   e. All of the above

4. Followers of Scientology:
   a. Obey the "True Parents."
   b. Try to get clear of engrams (hang-ups).
   c. Have faith in Bahá'u'lláh.
   d. Worship the Gohonzon scroll.

5. Of the following groups which one does not include a belief in reincarnation?
   a. New Age
   b. Hare Krishna
   c. Nation of Islam
   d. Buddhism
   e. Scientology

Discussion Questions

1. Why should Christians study other religions?
2. What stood out to you as you read through these various religious groups?
3. How much or how little experience have you had with these religious groups? Share about an experience or conversation with someone in any of these groups.
4. What differences and similarities do you notice between Christianity and the other faiths about who they say Jesus is?
5. What differences and similarities do you notice between Christianity and the other faiths about what "salvation" is, and what it takes to be "saved"?

CHRISTIANITY, CULTS & THE OCCULT

Worksheet

1. Which group is a form of Jewish mysticism and extra-biblical revelation?
   - a. Kabbalah Centre
   - b. Freemasonry
   - c. Wicca
   - d. Santería

2. Which animistic religion's followers must appease many unpredictable spirits—including the spirits of the dead?
   - a. Satanism
   - b. Theosophy
   - c. Eckankar
   - d. Santería

3. Which group was started in London as a lodge and omits references to Jesus when quoting the Bible?
   - a. Freemasonry
   - b. Rosicrucianism
   - c. Anthroposophy
   - d. Theosophy

4. Which of the following is <u>not</u> true about astrology?
   - a. It is condemned in the Bible.
   - b. It is a form of divination.
   - c. It is another name for astronomy.
   - d. It seems to offer people an explanation for their troubles.

5. Which group is known for conducting séances to contact the dead and using the Ouija® board?
   - a. Wicca
   - b. Astrology
   - c. Spiritualism
   - d. Rosicrucianism

Discussion Questions

1. As you read this chapter, which groups were you familiar with, and which ones were new to you?
2. Read Acts 8:9–24. How is the power of the Holy Spirit through Philip, Peter, and John different from the sorcery of Simon?
3. Occult practices are condemned many times in the Bible. What do you think are some reasons why God so strongly forbids his people from practicing the occult?
4. What makes astrology and horoscopes appealing? What does Jesus offer us instead?
5. How is the gospel of Jesus good news for people involved in the occult?

CHRISTIANITY & EASTERN RELIGIONS

Worksheet

1. *Pantheism*, a bedrock of eastern religious philosophy, literally means:
   a. Many gods
   b. All is God
   c. No God
   d. None of the above

2. Salvation in eastern religions is:
   a. Having one's sins forgiven by God   c. Escaping the cycles of reincarnation
   b. Going to a heavenly paradise after death   d. Attaining physical health

3. In Buddha's teachings the idea of pursuing or knowing "God" is considered:
   a. A means of salvation   c. A valuable source of comfort
   b. Irrelevant and can hinder enlightenment   d. The way to immortality

4. Which religion is said to have as many as 33 million gods?
   a. Hinduism   c. Buddhism
   b. Sikhism   d. Confucianism

5. The Dalai Lama of Tibetan Buddhism said that Jesus:
   a. Lived previous lives.
   b. Used Buddhist practices.
   c. Was an enlightened person (bodhisattva).
   d. All of the above
   e. None of the above

Discussion Questions

1. After reading this chapter, what did you learn about eastern religions that you didn't know or understand before?
2. Share about a time that you had an interaction or conversation with someone in an eastern religion. What did you learn from that experience?
3. How would you describe Jesus of Christianity to someone who believes Jesus was a guru or an enlightened person (bodhisattva)?
4. How would you respond to someone who said, "Eastern religions and Christianity are just different paths to escaping pain and getting to God. They are basically the same."?
5. What difficulties and challenges do you think someone who is a follower of an eastern religion would face if he or she became a Christian?

ISLAM & CHRISTIANITY

Worksheet

1. True or False? Muslims also call Allah (God) "Our Father."

2. True or False? Muslims believe Jesus was a prophet appointed by Allah.

3. The greatest sin in Islam is *shirk* which means:
    a. To lie (bear false witness).
    b. To disrespect the Quran.
    c. To associate any partner with Allah (idolatry).
    d. To lose one's honor.

4. *Jihad* which means "holy struggle" can be:
    a. A struggle in the soul to do the right thing.
    b. An effort against the enemies of Islam.
    c. Both (a) and (b)
    d. None of the above

5. Which of the following do Muslims believe they must do to be saved?
    a. Do good deeds
    b. Practice the five pillars
    c. Trust Muhammad as savior
    d. a) and (b)
    e. All of the above

Discussion Questions

1. After reading this chapter, what did you learn about Islam that you didn't know or understand before?
2. Share about a time that you had an interaction or conversation with a Muslim. What did you learn from that experience?
3. How is salvation in Islamic teaching different than what Jesus taught about how to be saved?
4. How is the gospel of Jesus Christ good news for Muslims?
5. Read 1 Corinthians 9:19–23. How can you apply theses verses in your own conversations and interactions with Muslims?

10 Q&A ON JEHOVAH'S WITNESSES

Worksheet

1. Which of the following is <u>not</u> true about the doctrine of the Trinity?
   - a. The Trinity is the historic Christian view.
   - b. Father, Son, and Holy Spirit are three persons revealed in one God.
   - c. Jesus and the Father are the same person in different forms.
   - d. Each of the persons in the Trinity are called "God" in Scripture.

2. True or False? The Bible teaches that *everyone* who puts their faith in Christ is "born again" and has Jesus as their mediator.

3. The good works that people do:
   - a. Help earn salvation in addition to faith.
   - b. Can guarantee forgiveness of sin.
   - c. Are the root cause of a saved relationship with God.
   - d. Are evidence of a saved relationship with God.
   - e. None of the above

4. God's Word (the Bible):
   - a. Is most accurate in the New World Translation.
   - b. Is preserved sufficiently to convey God's revealed truth.
   - c. Has variations that support significantly different religious ideas.
   - d. Has lost many important parts because of poor transmission.
   - e. Both (a) and (b)

5. True or False? Jesus is called the firstborn because he was the first of God's created beings.

Discussion Questions

1. Share about a conversation you had with a Jehovah's Witness. What things were discussed? Was it easy or difficult to discuss different beliefs?
2. What do you think are some reasons for why people join the Jehovah's Witnesses?
3. What is required for someone to be "saved" in Jehovah's Witnesses teaching? What is required in Christianity?
4. What difficulties and challenges do you think someone would face if he or she left the Jehovah's Witnesses and became a Christian?
5. Do you feel ready to discuss your beliefs with Jehovah's Witnesses? Why or why not? What would help you feel ready?

10 Q&A ON MORMONISM

Worksheet

1. The Bible:
   a. Is "God-breathed."
   b. Has lost many of its "plain and precious parts."
   c. Is superseded by revelations from the living prophet.
   d. Has been extensively revised by corrupt transcribers.

2. True or False? Being made in the image of God means that humans can become Gods.

3. True or False? The blessing of being in God's presence and part of his family is a blessing that must be earned.

4. Which of the following is <u>not</u> true about humankind?
   a. Incapable of meeting the standard of perfection necessary to abide in God's presence.
   b. Are justified by faith.
   c. Will face either eternal condemnation or life in heaven.
   d. Pre-existed in heaven before becoming human.

5. True or False? The Book of Mormon is an ancient document.

Discussion Questions

1. Share about a conversation you had with a Mormon. What things were discussed? Was it easy or difficult to discuss different beliefs?
2. What do you think are some reasons for why people join the Mormon Church?
3. What was the purpose of Jesus' death and resurrection according to Mormonism? What was the purpose according to Christianity?
4. What difficulties and challenges do you think someone would face if he or she left the Mormon Church and became a Christian?
5. Do you feel ready to discuss your beliefs with Mormons? Why or why not? What would help you feel ready?

10 KEYS TO WITNESSING TO CULTS

Worksheet

1. Which three biblical doctrines do cults most often deny or distort?
     a. Trinity, Baptism, and Second Coming
     b. Creation, Jesus' deity, and Salvation
     c. Trinity, Jesus Christ, and Salvation
     d. Trinity, Jesus Christ, and Lord's Supper

2. When interpreting Scripture remember to:
     a. Always examine the context.
     b. Examine a verse in light of clear passages.
     c. Draw meaning out of the verses.
     d. (a) and (b)
     e. All of the above

3. True or False? Cult groups sometimes get the identity of Jesus wrong.

4. What do cultists need to hear about more than anything else?
     a. Their sinfulness
     b. The Bible's authority
     c. Christian history
     d. God's grace
     e. Spiritual deception

5. True of False? Because ex-cultists are hungry for something to believe in, you should make sure that they immediately join and attend your church.

Discussion Questions

1. Read Galatians 1:6–9. Why do you think Scripture speaks so strongly against false teachers?
2. Before reading this chapter, did you think of Jehovah's Witnesses or Mormonism as a cult? Why or why not.
3. Do you think it is helpful to tell people they are in a cult? Why or why not?
4. In your own words, how would you explain the gospel of Jesus Christ?
5. Have you given your testimony to someone in a cult or to a non-Christian? What was easy or difficult about it? What was the person's response?
6. First Peter 3:15 tells us to "Always be prepared to give an answer to everyone who asks you to give the reason for the hope that you have." What are some things you can do to better prepare yourself?

FEEDBACK

1. What did you learn through this study that deepened your relationship with God and/or helped you understand biblical teachings better?

_____

_____

2. What was your favorite thing about this study, and why?

_____

_____

3. How could the meeting location, setting, length, or time be improved?

_____

_____

4. Did you think the material covered was too difficult, too easy, or just right?

_____

_____

5. What would you like to see different about the group discussions?

_____

_____

6. What would you like to see different about the worksheets?

_____

_____

7. What topic would you like to learn more about?

_____

_____

Look for Other Rose Bible Basics Books

Free, downloadable study guide at rose-publishing.com.
Click on "News & Info," then on "Downloads."

The Bible at a Glance

This introduction to basic Bible knowledge contains: a Bible overview summarizing each book of the Bible in 100 words or less, a Bible time line comparing Bible history and world history side by side, an introduction to studying the Bible, Then & Now Bible Maps, where to find favorite Bible verses, Bible promises, the basics of the Christian life, and a Bible translations comparison chart.

112 pages, 6 x 9-inch paperback.   ISBN: 9781596362000

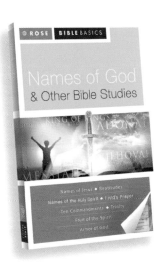

Names of God and Other Bible Studies

Contains favorite Bible studies to use in small groups, church groups, and for individual study. Includes studies on the Names of God, Names of Jesus, Names of the Holy Spirit, Trinity, Ten Commandments, Lord's Prayer, Beatitudes, Fruit of the Spirit, and Armor of God. 112 pages. Includes color charts, illustrations, and photos throughout.

128 pages, 6 x 9-inch paperback.   ISBN: 9781596362031

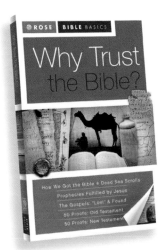

Why Trust the Bible?

Is the Bible an ancient document that has been tampered with? Has it been edited many times over the centuries and now is filled with errors? How can we know what the Bible really said when the originals no longer exist?

This book gives answers to the following claims by critics:
- The Gospels were written long after Jesus lived by people who weren't eyewitnesses.
- The stories about Jesus' life and death were not handed down reliably and not recorded accurately.
- The Bible is full of textual errors, as proven by the Dead Sea Scrolls.
- The New Testament wasn't finalized until hundreds of years after Jesus and his disciples, so there could have been many other "Gospels" accepted and later rejected in addition to the four Gospels found in the Bible today.
- The Bible was edited by people who had an "agenda" and changed many teachings.

128 pages, 6 x 9-inch paperback.   ISBN: 9781596362017

Other Rose Publishing Books

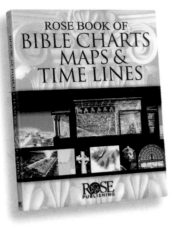

Rose Book of Bible Charts, Maps & Time Lines

Dozens of popular Rose Publishing Bible charts, maps, and time lines in one spiral-bound book. Reproduce up to 300 copies of any chart free of charge.

192 pages. Hardcover.   ISBN-13: 9781596360228

Deluxe "Then and Now" Bible Maps
Book with CD-ROM!
See where Bible places are today with "Then and Now" Bible maps with clear plastic overlays of modern cities and countries. This deluxe edition comes with a CD-ROM that gives you a JPG of each map to use in your own Bible material as well as PDFs of each map and overlay to create your own handouts or overhead transparencies. PowerPoint fans can create their own presentations with these digitized maps.

Hardcover. ISBN-13: 9781596361638

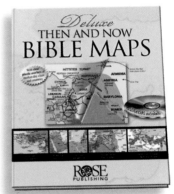

Rose Book of Bible & Christian History Time Lines
Six thousand years and 20 feet of time lines in one hard-bound cover! This unique resource allows you to easily store and reference two time lines in book form. These gorgeous time lines printed on heavy chart paper, can also be slipped out of their binding and posted in a hallway or large room for full effoot.
• The 10-foot Bible Time Line compares Scriptural events with world history and Middle East history. Shows hundreds of facts; includes dates of kings, prophets, battles, and key events.
• The 10-foot Christian History Time Line begins with the life of Jesus and continues to the present day. Includes key people and events that all Christians should know. Emphasis on world missions, the expansion of Christianity, and Bible translation in other languages. These two time lines are connected end-to-end to form one long teaching aid.

Hardcover. ISBN-13: 9781596360846